At Issue

What Rights Should Illegal Immigrants Have?

Other Books in the At Issue Series:

Age of Consent

Biodiversity

Can Busy Teens Succeed Academically?

Can Celebrities Change the World?

Club Drugs

Does the U.S. Two-Party System Still Work?

How Safe Is America's Infrastructure?

Nuclear Weapons

The Olympics

Polygamy

Teen Smoking

Teen Suicide

The U.S. Policy on Cuba

What Is the Future of the Music Industry?

What Is the Impact of E-Waste?

What Is the Impact of Tourism?

What Role Should the U.S. Play in the Middle East?

At Issue

What Rights Should Illegal Immigrants Have?

Noël Merino, Book Editor

GREENHAVEN PRESS
A part of Gale, Cengage Learning

GALE
CENGAGE Learning™

Detroit • New York • San Francisco • New Haven, Conn • Waterville, Maine • London

Christine Nasso, *Publisher*
Elizabeth Des Chenes, *Managing Editor*

© 2010 Greenhaven Press, a part of Gale, Cengage Learning.

Gale and Greenhaven Press are registered trademarks used herein under license.

For more information, contact:
Greenhaven Press
27500 Drake Rd.
Farmington Hills, MI 48331-3535
Or you can visit our Internet site at gale.cengage.com

For product information and technology assistance, contact us at

Gale Customer Support, 1-800-877-4253
For permission to use material from this text or product, submit all requests online at
www.cengage.com/permissions

Further permissions questions can be e-mailed to permissionrequest@cengage.com

Articles in Greenhaven Press anthologies are often edited for length to meet page requirements. In addition, original titles of these works are changed to clearly present the main thesis and to explicitly indicate the author's opinion. Every effort is made to ensure that Greenhaven Press accurately reflects the original intent of the authors. Every effort has been made to trace the owners of copyrighted material.

Cover Image copyright © Images.com/Corbis.

LIBRARY OF CONGRESS CATALOGING-IN-PUBLICATION DATA

What rights should illegal immigrants have? / Noël Merino, book editor.
  p. cm. -- (At issue)
  Includes bibliographical references and index.
  ISBN 978-0-7377-4902-1 (hardcover) -- ISBN 978-0-7377-4903-8 (pbk.)
  1. Illegal aliens--United States--Juvenile literature. I. Merino, Noël.
  KF4819.85.W48 2010
  342.7308'3--dc22
                                                      2010004546

Printed in the United States of America
3 4 5 6 7 14 13 12 11 10

Contents

Introduction   7

1. Enforcing Existing Immigration Law   11
   Violates Rights of Illegal Immigrants
   National Network for Immigrant and
   Refugee Rights

2. Existing Immigration Law Should Be Enforced   23
   Alex Alexiev

3. Employer Sanctions for Hiring Illegal   29
   Immigrants Should Be Ended
   Bill Ong Hing and David Bacon

4. Immigration Raids Are Justified Because   34
   Lawbreakers Are Criminals
   William P. Hoar

5. Immigration Raids Turn Victims into   40
   Criminals and Violate Worker Rights
   Danielle Maestretti

6. Immigration Raids Justify Counter   45
   Exploitation of Illegal Immigrants
   Jamie Glazov

7. Illegal Immigrants Should Not Be   51
   Allowed Amnesty
   Christopher M. Jaarda

8. Ethical Considerations Support Amnesty   59
   for Illegal Immigrants
   David DeCosse

9. Earned Legalization Is Preferable to   65
   Enforcement by Deportation
   Patricia Hatch and Katherine Fennelly

10. Illegal Alien Criminals Should Be Removed   71
    from the Country
    Jessica Vaughan and James R. Edwards, Jr.

11. Illegal Immigrants Should Not Be Able   75
    to Get Driver's Licenses
    Numbers USA

12. Children of Illegal Aliens Should Go to College 80
    and Gain Legal Status
    David Bennion

13. Children of Illegal Aliens Should Not Go   84
    to College and Gain Legal Status
    Yeh Ling-Ling

Organizations to Contact   88
Bibliography   94
Index   99

Introduction

Illegal immigration continues to be an issue of controversy, with an estimated 12 million unauthorized immigrants living in the United States, according to a 2008 report by the Pew Hispanic Center, a project of the Pew Research Center.[1] A 2009 study by the Pew Hispanic Center estimated that there were 8.3 million undocumented workers in the U.S. labor force in March 2008, with unauthorized immigrant workers accounting for 5.4 percent of the U.S. workforce. With these high numbers of illegal immigrants living and working within the United States, it is no wonder that people from all political backgrounds are calling for immigration reform. Central to the issue of reform is the question of what kinds of rights illegal immigrants should have.

There are a couple of ways that people end up becoming illegal immigrants in the United States. For many individuals, entrance to the United States is first granted legally through a valid work visa or visitor visa, but after such a visa expires the individual may fail to leave the country, taking up residence illegally. It is also the case that some people cross the borders illegally without ever gaining legal access through a work or visitor visa. In each of these two manners of becoming an illegal immigrant, a law is broken either by failing to respect the terms of a visa or by failing to gain legal entry.

The fact that people become illegal immigrants by breaking the law has led some to insist that all illegal immigrants are criminals and should not have rights of any sort but, rather, should be deported as soon as their legal status is detected. The Federation for American Immigration Reform (FAIR) advocates this position and believes that ending illegal immigration requires that illegal immigrants "not be able to

1. Pew Hispanic Center, www.pewhispanic.org.

obtain employment, public assistance benefits, public education, public housing, or any other taxpayer-funded benefit."[2]
Other groups believe that illegal immigrants already in the
country should be given a path to citizenship alongside immigration reform: The National Immigration Forum advocates
the creation of a "rigorous registration process" for illegal immigrants currently in the United States "that leads to lawful
permanent resident status and eventual citizenship."[3] There is
wide disagreement about what should be done about illegal
immigrants already in the United States, not to mention the
disagreement about policies governing immigration in the future.

A complicating factor in the illegal immigrant debate involves the children of illegal immigrants. Normally, children
born in the United States to illegal immigrant children will be
granted U.S. citizenship. Many illegal immigrant children are
brought to the United States by their parents, however. Unlike
their parents, they cannot rightfully be said to have broken
the law on their own accord. One example of how the United
States has approached the rights of the children of illegal immigrants is illustrative of the ongoing debate about the rights
of illegal immigrants.

One major controversy regarding the rights of illegal immigrants involves the public education of illegal immigrant
children. This issue was legally resolved in 1982 by the U.S.
Supreme Court, although the decision was not popular with
everyone and continues to be condemned by some. The 1982
case of *Plyler v. Doe* involved a Texas law that withheld state
funds from educating illegal immigrant children, permitting
school districts to deny these children enrollment. Up until
the decision in *Plyler*, it was understood that all children re-

2. Federation for American Immigration Reform (FAIR), "Illegal Immigration Is a
Crime," March 2005. www.fairus.org. http://www.fairus.org/site/News2?page=NewsArticle
&id=16663&security=1601&news_iv_ctrl=1007.
3. Rich Stolz, Campaign to Reform Immigration for America, "Immigration Reform in
the 111th Congress: Principles of Immigration Reform," National Immigration Forum,
2009. www.immigrationforum.org.

siding in the United States legally have a right to a public education. The Court in *Plyler* determined that there was no good justification for any state to withhold this right from children who were brought into the United States illegally by their parents, finding the Equal Protection Clause of the Fourteenth Amendment to protect illegal immigrant children from unequal treatment without respect to public education.

Since this decision, all states have had to provide illegal immigrant children access to the same public education system to which legal resident children have access. According to the Pew Hispanic Center, illegal immigrants' children (themselves both citizens and noncitizens) constitute 6.8 percent of students in U.S. elementary and secondary schools. Many who oppose this policy argue that offering free public education to the children of illegal immigrants encourages people to break the law and is unfair to American taxpayers, as such a policy obviously created extra costs for the states. There is a similar controversy regarding a current proposal to create a path to legal residency for illegal immigrant children who graduate from U.S. high schools. The Development, Relief, and Education for Alien Minors Act (DREAM Act) would allow illegal immigrants who pursue legal residency under the act to have access to student loans, work-study programs, and in-state tuition rates at colleges. For the same reason that many oppose providing free public education to illegal immigrant children, the DREAM Act is also opposed as being unfair to legal residents.

The debate about what rights illegal immigrants should have goes well beyond the controversy of educating the children of illegal immigrants using taxpayers' money. There is disagreement about whether illegal immigrants should be deported or given amnesty; disagreement about whether places of employment should be raided in order to catch illegal immigrants; and disagreement about whether illegal immigrants should be given privileges such as driver's licenses. These are a few of the topics covered within the viewpoints included in *At Issue: What Rights Should Illegal Immigrants Have?*

1

Enforcing Existing Immigration Law Violates Rights of Illegal Immigrants

National Network for Immigrant and Refugee Rights

National Network for Immigrant and Refugee Rights is a national organization composed of local coalitions and immigrant, refugee, community, religious, civil rights, and labor organizations working to defend and expand the rights of all immigrants and refugees, regardless of immigration status.

Government entities, law enforcement agencies, and employers are committing rights violations against immigrants and refugees in the United States. There has been a marked increase in immigration raids and other immigration enforcement operations in recent years, which has had negative effects on communities, immigrant workers, and children. The practice of detaining undocumented immigrants has increased as well, and there are concerns about the treatment of detainees within these detainment facilities. The federal government's militarization of the border between the United States and Mexico is resulting in deaths of immigrants, and extension of a border fence will make the problem worse without decreasing the number of undocumented immigrants. Overall, current U.S. immigration policy is causing a humanitarian crisis.

National Network for Immigrant and Refugee Rights, "Over-Raided, Under Siege: U.S. Immigration Laws and Enforcement Destroy the Rights of Immigrants," January 2008, pp. 1, 4–6, 12–13, 24–26, 47. Reproduced by permission of the National Network for Immigrant and and Refugee Rights.

Analyzing [more than] 100 stories of abuse and 206 incidents of immigration raids during 2006–2007, *Over-Raided, Under Siege* found recurring patterns of rights violations perpetrated against immigrants and refugees by government entities, law enforcement agencies and employers. The most alarming trend, and by far the most prevalent in the last two years [2006–2007], is the increase in immigration sweeps by ICE [U.S. Immigration and Customs Enforcement] at people's homes and in their workplaces. The raids, in turn, have led to a rising demand for detention facilities that house immigrants awaiting deportation orders. Recent reports point to dismal health and living conditions at these facilities, many of which are run by private prison firms. . . .

Meanwhile, Congress continues to inflate the DHS's [Department of Homeland Security] ICE and CBP [U.S. Customs and Border Protection] budgets for militarizing the southwest border region, linking it to the intensification of interior enforcement. This consists of laws, practices, policies and new proposals increasing policing, wall building and incarceration of immigrants and a growing reliance on private security corporations. The federal government's strategies and conduct have fueled the mounting number of local, county and state law enforcement agencies and governments that have jumped on the enforcement bandwagon—collaborating with immigration authorities—and are destabilizing communities and putting them under great risk.

ICE Raids

The criminalization of immigrant workers reached new heights with two turning points, setting the stage for an aggressive attack on immigrants by the Department of Homeland Security. First, the U.S. House of Representatives passed the notorious Sensenbrenner bill (HR 4437) on December 16, 2005. This bill made it a felony to be undocumented and to assist, hire, minister to or provide services to the undocumented. In reaction to the Sensenbrenner bill, immigrant communities and allies organized unprecedented mass mobilizations to reject HR 4437 and call for socially just immigration reform.

As the size and frequency of the mobilizations grew, the Department of Homeland Security began unleashing a series of highly publicized ICE raids. In April 2006, ICE carried out wide-scale immigration raids against workers at IFCO Systems plants [that provide food transport services] in forty locations across eight states that led to the deportation of over 1,100 people.

Then on December 12, 2006, U.S. Immigration and Customs Enforcement (ICE) carried out the "Swift" raids, one of the largest immigration sweeps in history, clamping down on immigrant workers in meatpacking plants across six states. The Swift factories came to a standstill as some 12,000 Swift plant workers were rounded up, detained and questioned about their status on site. Despite this massive use of force, ICE charged only 65 workers, mostly on felony charges of identity theft and fraud for using false social security numbers. The United Food and Commercial Workers Union, which represents five of the six sites raided, has filed a lawsuit against ICE to protect Fourth Amendment rights and stop the U.S. government "from illegally arresting and detaining workers, including U.S. citizens and legal residents while at their workplace."

In FY [fiscal year] 2006, these ICE raids and other immigration enforcement operations led to the deportation of 221,664 undocumented immigrants, a 20 percent increase from the previous year. Despite protests from civil and human rights leaders, this modus operandi only continued in 2007. The stepped-up-raids strategy and corresponding increase in detentions, deportations and policing is at the center of Operation Endgame, a ten-year campaign laid out by the DHS in 2003 to track down and deport all immigrants, documented and undocumented, who can be deported. The following are just three examples of how ICE has stepped up its raids strategy:

> On March 29, 2007, federal agents detained 69 undocumented immigrants hired by a Baltimore temporary employment agency. That same month, ICE agents arrested 327 employees working for Michael Bianco, Inc, a leather goods manufacturer in New Bedford, Massachusetts. The raid left 140 children stranded. Most of the immigrants arrested were Guatemalans who had fled civil war in their home country in the 1980s. During a two-week period in September 2007, ICE agents carried out the largest raid in the nation. They arrested more than 1,300 immigrants and deported 530 from five Southern California counties: Los Angeles (187), Orange (62), Riverside/San Bernardino (245), and Ventura (36). The majority of these were bystanders, "collateral" arrests, swept up by ICE as they executed orders of deportation for others. The deportees came to the U.S. from various nations, including Mexico, El Salvador, Honduras, Ireland and Russia.

As ICE launches more aggressive raids, an alarming number of children are being left behind without their parents.

Concerns About Raids

The timing of ICE raids over the past few years raises many troubling questions about the DHS's accountability and political motivations. Just as ICE launched the IFCO raids shortly after the mass mobilizations of 2006, the bureau has continued to conduct raids following local and national efforts to promote immigrant rights. In New Haven, Connecticut, immigration authorities swept up 31 undocumented immigrants just two days after the city approved a municipal identification card that will all allow city residents, regardless of their citizenship status, to access basic city services. "We feel that this is too much to be a coincidence; this is a retaliation," said Jessica Mayorga, spokeswoman for New Haven mayor John DeStefano Jr. "They are attacking us because they failed to integrate immigration reform that worked. That's not our fault, and we're doing everything we can to protect the immigrants of New Haven."

Increasingly, the workplace has become the preferred raid location. According to ICE, 4,000 people were arrested in workplace raids between October 2006 and September 2007. The previous fiscal year, the number reached 3,700. These figures represent an astounding 800 percent increase since 2003, when agents arrested fewer than 500 people.

ICE agents increasingly have gone door-to-door looking for immigrants with deportation orders, using the pretext of a warrant for one undocumented immigrant to arrest many others. Often, they failed to find the person for whom they had issued a deportation order. In the case of the New Haven raids, federal immigration agents went searching for 16 undocumented immigrants with arrest warrants. Only four warrants were served, meaning that the majority of the people taken into custody were swept up in a dragnet. Marc Raimondi, an ICE spokesperson, glossing over how ICE made these arrests, stated, "There is truly no safe haven for fugitive aliens."

As ICE launches more aggressive raids, an alarming number of children are being left behind without their parents. Studies estimate that between 3.1 million children and 5 million children—who are U.S. citizens—are living with at least one undocumented immigrant parent. While these children cannot be deported, having their parents rounded up by immigration authorities leaves them vulnerable to family separation, economic hardship and psychological trauma.

In October 2007, ICE was holding 14,764 immigrants in detention facilities throughout the nation. The practice of de-

taining undocumented immigrants and asylum seekers awaiting removal proceedings has skyrocketed in the past decade.
The National Immigration Justice Center estimates that detentions have increased 400 percent from 5,532 in 1994 to 27,500
in 2006. On December 5, 2007, the Department of Justice reported that last year immigration detention had the greatest
growth rate of all U.S. federal and state prison systems.

Massive changes in immigration law in the mid-90s and
increased enforcement after 9/11 fueled the surge. In 1996,
Congress passed the Illegal Immigration Reform and Immigrant Responsibility Act (IIRIRA), which made sweeping
changes to immigration law. It required mandatory detentions
of undocumented immigrants and asylum seekers, and took
away the discretion of INS [Immigration and Naturalization
Service] agents and even judges to release people that posed
no security threat or flight risk. After September 11, the pre-
carious link between immigration and terrorism accelerated
the enforcement strategy to include more detentions. Since
9/11, the number of detainees has risen 40 percent.

One of the alarming shifts in immigration control has
been the privatization of immigrant detention centers, both in
the construction and operation of its facilities. Currently, ICE
runs eight detention facilities known as Service Processing
Centers and relies on state and local jails and federal prisons
for additional bed space. Despite access to these facilities,
ICE's increased detention figures have led to contracts with
the nation's largest private prison operators to run eight additional detention facilities. The federal government pays these
corporations roughly $180 a day per person detained. Correc-
tions Corporation of America and the Geo Group (formerly
the Wackenhut Corrections Corporation) house almost 20
percent of the immigrants in detention. These and other com-
panies are looking to corner the market as the detention business grows.

The Drive for Profit

Part of this lucrative business is the construction of detention centers. In February 2006, the Army Corps of Engineers awarded a $385 million contract for constructing immigration detention centers to Kellogg Brown & Root, the Halliburton subsidiary that has been criticized for overcharging the Pentagon for its services in Iraq (e.g. cooking, construction, power generation and fuel transportation).

U.S. immigration control strategies have turned the border into the epicenter of a human rights crisis.

As the apparent drive for profit has led detention facility managers to cut corners, conditions inside these facilities raise grave concerns. In 2006, the Office of the Inspector General conducted an audit of five detention facilities used by U.S. Immigration and Customs Enforcement (ICE). The federal government audit found multiple instances of non-compliance with detention standards related to health care, environmental health and safety, general conditions of confinement, and the reporting of abuse. Interviews with detainees revealed pest control problems (rats, insects and vermin), facilities with poor ventilation, rape and abusive search allegations, as well as inadequate procedures for reporting civil rights violations. Recent reports of detainees dying while in federal immigration custody have also highlighted the severity of the problem. In August 2007, the *Washington Post* reported the death of three detainees—a pregnant Mexican woman, an AIDS patient, and a Brazilian with a history of epileptic seizures. Witnesses say that in two of these cases, ICE authorities refused to give detainees adequate medical treatment. Since 2004, at least 62 people have died in ICE custody.

Another aspect of this trend will continue to deepen as DHS begins to extend a pilot project along the border; this project requires jailing all immigrants for periods ranging from thirty-four days to six months for a first-time unauthorized entry before deporting them. First implemented in the Del Rio sector of the Texas border with Mexico in [2005], "Operation Streamline" represents an immigration policing collaboration with state and local prosecutors. Second and repeat unauthorized entries can result in jail sentences of two or more years. Operation Streamline has had the effect of pushing migrants further west into Arizona's most desolate and dangerous desert and mountainous region. More migrants will be jailed, labeled "criminals" subject to punitive imprisonment, and more migrants will die as a result of this "deterrent" to crossing without a visa. . . .

The United States–Mexico Border

The United States–Mexico border stretches 2,000 miles long, from the Pacific Ocean to the Gulf of Mexico. The remote terrain varies from mountainous peaks to expanses of brutal desert. Long an area where people, wildlife and livestock crossed freely, U.S. immigration control strategies have turned the border into the epicenter of a human rights crisis. They force migrants to risk their lives by crossing through the most desolate and hazardous terrain of the border region.

Despite continuing an enforcement strategy that has failed to curtail unauthorized migration, the U.S. government continues to invest billions of dollars every year in the border build-up that is deepening border militarization and extending it into interior enforcement. DHS plans include doubling the number of U.S. Border Patrol agents and tripling the number of interior ICE agents. In February 2007, President [George W.] Bush requested roughly $13 billion for border controls and internal enforcement of immigration laws for FY 2008. His proposal [represented] a $3 billion increase from FY 2007. In August 2007, Homeland Security Secretary Michael Chertoff and Commerce Secretary Carlos Gutierrez announced a series of new border enforcement measures. By the end of

2008, DHS aims to increase the number of Border Patrol agents from 15,000 to 18,300 (this figure represents a doubling of Border Patrol agents under the Bush administration). The initiative will also add 370 miles of fencing, 300 vehicle barriers, 105 camera and radar towers and 3 unmanned aerial vehicles.

As the federal government increases the militarization of the border, authorities recover increasing numbers of deceased migrants each year. Human rights groups that monitor migrant deaths at the border believe that for every migrant body recovered at least ten others are missing or dead in the remote deserts and mountains.

According to the U.S. Border Patrol, 1,954 people died crossing the U.S.-Mexico border between the years 1998–2004. In FY 2005, facing a summer of triple-digit heat, a record-breaking 473 migrants died at the border; 279 of these individuals died on the Arizona border. Coalición de Derechos Humanos in Tucson [Arizona] has reported that 1,327 migrants perished crossing the Arizona U.S.-Mexico border between October of 2001 and September of 2007. Most victims died from dehydration or hyperthermia. Others drowned in the strong currents of border canals and rivers as they tried bypassing the worst of the desert. A significant number died in motor vehicle accidents.

U.S. Border Control Strategy

In spite of the overwhelming evidence that the militarization of immigration and border control is failing to dissuade unauthorized crossings, the U.S. government continues expanding a strategy meant to deliberately cause suffering and the death of migrants who have no other option than risking their lives to reunite with loved ones and to work. On September 19, 1993—just weeks before Congress ratified the North American Free Trade Agreement (NAFTA)—the [President Bill] Clinton Administration implemented "Operation

Blockade" along the El Paso sector of the U.S.-Mexico border. The "prevention through deterrence" strategy consisted of placing one Border Patrol agent and vehicle every thousand yards over a 20-mile mile stretch between Ysleta, Texas, and Sunland Park, New Mexico.

In 1994, the U.S. government extended the "prevention through deterrence" strategy to the entire border, first launching "Operation Gatekeeper," an initiative aimed at blocking traditional crossing routes along the California [portion of the] U.S.-Mexico border. Operation Gatekeeper was touted as a success, having reduced the number of apprehensions along the California border by 20 percent between 1994 and 2000. But these figures only tell half the story.

The construction and continuing extension of the border "fence," increased high-tech surveillance, and thousands of additional Border Patrol agents stationed along the southwest border have done nothing to stop the number of unauthorized migrants crossing into the United States. Rather, the almost 15-year-old strategy of border controls has closed off traditional points of entry and funneled thousands of migrants through the deadliest stretches of border desert and mountains, where they risk their lives and are left at the mercy of unscrupulous smugglers and vigilantes. Between 1994 and 2000, immigrant apprehensions rose 55 percent in Texas and 351 percent in Arizona. The Pima County [Arizona] Medical Examiner's Office (PCMEO), which handles 90 percent of all unauthorized border-crossing bodies in the U.S. Border Patrol's Tucson Sector, saw a sharp spike in deaths around the same period of time.

In December 2005, the Department of Homeland Security introduced another border control pilot project, "Operation Streamline," in the Del Rio, Texas sector. Under Operation Streamline, every undocumented migrant detained will be automatically jailed and prosecuted.

Since DHS launched Operation Streamline, over 23,000 migrants have been prosecuted, and 22,000 have been convicted and deported. The courts typically charge first-time offenders with a misdemeanor, punishable by up to 180 days in jail and deportation. In Del Rio, the average jail time for first-time offenders has been 34 days. A second-time offense could mean up to two years in prison and deportation. Third-time offenders face even harsher sentences and deportation. Like Operation Blockade, its 1993 precursor, Operation Streamline is pushing migrants deeper into mountainous areas where not even Border Patrol all-terrain vehicles can enter. . . .

Human Rights Violations

The Human Rights Immigrant Community Action Network (HURRICANE) has documented consistent patterns of abuse and human rights violations by the U.S. government, local, county and state governments, employers and private citizen groups. The escalation of raids, detentions and deportations, worker exploitation, an increasingly militarized border, and mounting collaboration between ICE and local law enforcement agencies have wreaked havoc on immigrant and refugee communities.

The Department of Homeland Security has relentlessly curtailed the rights of immigrants, especially the undocumented.

Unless public officials begin to reverse and make deep changes to U.S. immigration policies, laws and strategies, we will continue to witness an out-of-control humanitarian crisis within our borders. Migrant deaths and disappearances will continue to rise at the border. Undocumented workers will be left with few choices but to continue working for less than a living wage and be subjected to abhorrent conditions. Communities will feel less secure as immigrants and refugees avoid approaching police officers with crime-solving information for fear of detection and deportation. In addition, families will continue to be forced apart as immigration policies criminalize and deport people whose only offense was not having the proper documents.

Over-Raided, Under Siege: U.S. Immigration Laws and Enforcement Destroy the Rights of Immigrants exposes the scapegoating of immigrants as a new type of collective punishment, rooted in the further militarization of immigration and border control and the unprecedented criminalization of immigrants. Leading the way, the Department of Homeland Security has relentlessly curtailed the rights of immigrants, especially the undocumented, subjecting them to detention and deportation with impunity. Combining immigration control and national security, federal, state, county and local governments are imposing anti-immigrant measures as part of social and economic policies to privatize and cut back public services. They undermine community health and safety, marginalize and make immigrants more vulnerable to abuse and gut civil liberties.

The U.S. government's insistence on framing issues of migration as law enforcement and national security matters has prevented acknowledging and addressing the negative displacement impacts and involuntary migration of workers caused by economic restructuring, particularly the North American Free Trade Agreement (NAFTA). As long as the root causes of migration are denied and ignored, the U.S. will continue to block economically sustainable development for communities in sending countries, which would ameliorate and eventually decrease migration.

Over-Raided Under Siege urges the restoration and expansion of rights to stop and overturn this growing catastrophic state of affairs. Additionally, the U.S. government must address the root causes of migration by upholding and protecting human rights and implementing sustainable economic development.

2

Existing Immigration Law Should Be Enforced

Alex Alexiev

Alex Alexiev is an adjunct fellow at Hudson Institute and con-tributing editor for Family Security Matters, an organization that works to engage American families in America's security.

The high level of immigration by uneducated, unskilled, and il-literate people to California is having negative effects. Many of these immigrants are Latino and make up a sizable population in California's schools. Despite access to education, the attri-tion—or dropout—rates are high for Latinos who speak English as a second language. These dropouts end up costing the state money, not to mention failing to add any value to the economy. In order to stop the negative effects of poor immigrants, the ex-isting immigration law must be enforced, including the elimina-tion of welfare benefits for illegal aliens and the punishment of employers who hire illegal aliens.

California's financial unraveling has prompted a long-overdue debate about taxes, regulation, and government spending, but the state's media and government continue to ignore what could be an even greater problem: the irreparable damage to California's human capital that nearly 30 years of unrestrained illegal immigration has achieved.

This is not an immigration problem, or even an illegal-immigration problem, per se. A strong case could be made

Alex Alexiev, "Catching Up to Mexico: Illegal Immigration Is Depleting California's Hu-man Capital and Ravaging Its Economy," *National Review*, vol. 61, August 24, 2009, p. 22. Copyright © 2009 by National Review, Inc., 215 Lexington Avenue, New York, NY 10016. Reproduced by permission.

that, in terms of educational achievement, industriousness, and entrepreneurial acumen, Asian immigrants to California have proven superior to white natives of the state. Therefore, if California were to experience a wave of mass immigration from Asia, its long-term economic prospects would be improved. Today's Hispanic immigrants would probably have the same effect if they came from the top 10 to 20 percent of their society—according to those same measures of human capital—rather than from its bottom rungs. But the influx has instead been composed mainly of the poorly educated, the unskilled, and the illiterate. Such immigrants will likely soon dominate the state's overall population and politics.

In 2005, the California K-12 school system was 48.5 percent Hispanic, compared with 30.9 percent white. By now it is above 50 percent Hispanic. Two-thirds of kindergarten students were Hispanic, most of them unable to speak English.

For a closer glimpse of what's in store for California, look at the Los Angeles Unified School District, the largest in California and the second largest in the country. Of its roughly 700,000 students, almost three-quarters are Hispanic, 8.9 percent are white, and 11.2 percent are black. More than half of the Latino students (about 300,000) are "English learners" and, depending on whether you believe the district or independent scholars, anywhere between a third and a half drop out of high school, following significant attrition [dropout] in middle school. A recent study by UC [University of California] Santa Barbara's California Dropout Research Project estimates that high-school dropouts in 2007 alone will cost the state $24.2 billion in future economic losses.

Even those who graduate aren't necessarily headed to success. According to one study, 69 percent of Latino high-school graduates "do not meet college requirements or satisfy prerequisites for most jobs that pay a living wage." It is difficult to see how the majority-Hispanic labor force of the future can provide the skills that the sophisticated Los Angeles economy demands. Already studies show that as many as 700,000 Los Angeles Latinos and some 65 percent of the city's illegal immigrants work in L.A.'s huge underground economy.

The Negative Impact of Immigration

The unhappy picture in Los Angeles is replicated to one degree or another across much of California and is taking a huge toll on the state's economic competitiveness and long-term prospects. California's educational system, once easily the best in the county, is today mired in mediocrity—near the bottom among the 50 states as judged by National Assessment of Educational Progress (NAEP) tests in math, science, reading, and writing. And for the first time in its history, California is experiencing an increase in adult illiteracy. In 2003, it had the highest adult illiteracy in the United States, 23 percent—nearly 50 percent higher than a decade earlier. In some counties (Imperial at 41 percent, Los Angeles at 33 percent) illiteracy approaches sub-Saharan [Africa] levels.

California and [the federal government] need to enforce existing immigration law.

Perhaps even more important than the collapse of educational achievement among the lower strata is a deterioration of the higher education that was for decades the basis of California's preeminence in science and technology. California currently ranks 40th among the 50 states in college-attendance rates, and it already faces a significant shortage of college graduates. Studies have shown that the economy will need 40 percent of its workers to be college-educated by 2020, compared with today's 32 percent. Given the aging white population (average age, 42), many of these new graduates will have to come from the burgeoning Latino immigrant population (average age, 26). By one estimate, this would require [a] tripling of the number of college-educated immigrants, an impossibility if current trends hold. The state's inability to improve the educational attainment of its residents will result in a "substantial decline in per capita income" and "place California last among the 50 states" by 2020, according to a study by the National Center for Higher Education Management Systems.

The mediocre education system, along with the unfriendly business climate and confiscatory tax regime, is driving educated, middle-class Californians out of the state. Between 2000 and 2005, more people with college degrees left California than came in, according to research by the Hewlett Foundation. Since then this trend has accelerated, and the state lost 2.2 million members of its young, educated, tax-paying middle class between 2004 and 2007. IRS [Internal Revenue Service] data show that of recent migrants from the Golden State to places like Texas and Oklahoma, who average 29 years of age, 58 percent have received at least some college education and 53 percent own their homes.

> *The most disingenuous myth about illegal immigrants is that they do not impose any cost on society.*

In short, we are witnessing a highly advanced and prosperous state, long endowed with superior human capital, turning into the exact opposite in just one generation. What can be done to stop this race to the bottom? The answer is simple: California and [the federal government] need to enforce existing immigration law. Unfortunately, it is difficult to convince the public that this is necessary, so deeply entrenched are myths about illegal immigration.

Myths About Immigrants

One myth is that because America is a country of immigrants and has successfully absorbed waves of immigration in the past, it can absorb this wave. But the argument neglects two key differences between past waves and the current influx. First, the immigrant population is more than double today what it was following the most massive previous immigration wave (that of the late 19th century). Second, and much more important, as scholars from the Manhattan Institute have shown, earlier immigrants were much more likely to bring with them useful skills. Some Hispanic immigrants certainly do integrate, but most do not. Research has shown that even after 20 years in the country, most illegal aliens (the overwhelming majority of whom are Hispanic) and their children remain poor, unskilled, and culturally isolated—they constitute a new permanent underclass.

Perhaps the most disingenuous myth about illegal immigrants is that they do not impose any cost on society. The reality is that even those who work—and half do not, according to the Pew Hispanic Center—cannot subsist on the wages they receive, and [they] depend on public assistance to a large degree. Research on Los Angeles immigrants by Harvard University scholar George J. Borjas shows that 40.1 percent of immigrant families with non-citizen heads of household receive welfare, compared with 12.7 percent of households with native-born heads. Illegal immigrants also increase public expenditures on health care, education, and prisons. In California today, illegal immigrants' cost to the taxpayer is estimated to be $13 billion—half the state's budget deficit.

The state should stop providing welfare and other social services to illegal aliens—as existing statutes demand—and severely punish employers who break the law by hiring illegal immigrants. This would immediately remove powerful economic incentives for illegal immigration, and millions of illegal aliens would return to their countries. Instead, with President [Barack] Obama in the White House and the Democrats controlling Congress, an amnesty for the country's 13 million illegal immigrants may be soon to come.

[American economist] Milton Friedman once said that unrestrained immigration and the welfare state do not mix. Must we wait until California catches up with Mexico to realize how right he was?

3

Employer Sanctions for Hiring Illegal Immigrants Should Be Ended

Bill Ong Hing and David Bacon

Bill Ong Hing is a professor of law at University of California, Davis. He was on a United Food and Commercial Workers commission that examined the impact of the raids at Swift meatpacking plants, the largest workplace enforcement action in U.S. history. David Bacon, associate editor at Pacific News Service, is the author of several books on immigration—most recently, Illegal People: How Globalization Creates Migration and Criminalizes Immigrants.

For more than two decades, the hiring of undocumented workers has been prohibited. Employer sanctions, which are used to enforce this prohibition, are not working and are having negative effects on all workers. The strategy of employer sanctions has failed because the real problem is poverty in countries such as Mexico, which pressures people to flee to richer countries to support their families. Only with a change to trade and economic policies that put an end to poverty will people stop migrating to the United States in an attempt to remedy extreme poverty. All workers, including undocumented immigrant workers, need to be able to assert their labor rights and form unions. Employer sanctions should be ended, and a more generous policy for residence and family-reunification visas should be implemented.

Bill Ong Hing and David Bacon, "Rights, Not Raids," *The Nation*, vol. 288, May 18, 2009, p. 4. Copyright © 2009 The Nation. Reproduced by permission.

When the [President Barack] Obama administration reiterated recently that it will make an immigration reform proposal this year [2009], hopes rose among millions of immigrant families for the "change we can believe in." That was followed by a new immigration position embraced by both the AFL-CIO [American Federation of Labor and Congress of Industrial Organizations] and the Change to Win unions, rejecting the expansion of guest worker programs, which some unions had supported.

As it prepares a reform package, the administration should look seriously at why the deals created over the past several years failed, and consider alternatives. Beltway [Washington, D.C.] groups are again proposing employment visas for future (post-recession, presumably) labor shortages and continued imprisonment of the undocumented in detention centers, which they deem "necessary in some cases." Most disturbing, after years of the [George W.] Bush raids, is the continued emphasis on enforcement against workers.

We need a reality check.

Employer Sanctions

For more than two decades it has been a crime for an undocumented worker to hold a job in the United States. To enforce the prohibition, agents conduct immigration raids of the kind we saw at meatpacking plants in the past few years.

Today, some suggest "softer," or more politically palatable, enforcement—a giant database of Social Security numbers (E-Verify). Employers would be able to hire only those whose numbers "verify" their legal immigration status. Workers without such "work authorization" would have to be fired.

Whether hard or soft, these measures all enforce a provision of immigration law on the books since 1986—employer sanctions—which makes it illegal for an employer to hire a worker with no legal immigration status. In reality, the law makes it a crime for an undocumented worker to have a job.

The rationale has always been that this will dry up jobs for the undocumented and discourage them from coming. Those of us who served on a United Food and Commercial Workers commission that studied Immigration and Customs Enforcement (ICE) raids at Swift meatpacking plants across the country learned that the law has had disastrous effects on all workers. Instead of reinforcing or tweaking employer sanctions, we would be much better off if we ended them.

Raids and workplace enforcement have left severe emotional scars on families. Workers were mocked. Children were separated from their parents and left without word at schools or daycare. Increased enforcement has poisoned communities, spawning scores of state and local anti-immigrant laws and ordinances that target workers and their families.

A Failed Strategy

Employer sanctions have failed to reduce undocumented migration because NAFTA [North Atlantic Free Trade Agreement] and globalization create huge migration pressure. Since 1994 more than 6 million Mexicans have come to the United States. Ismael Rojas, who arrived without papers, says, "You can either abandon your children to make money to take care of them, or you can stay with your children and watch them live in misery. Poverty makes us leave our families."

Attempting to discourage workers from coming by arresting them for working without authorization, or trying to prevent them from finding work, is doomed to fail. To reduce the pressure that causes undocumented migration, we need to change our trade and economic policies so they don't produce poverty in countries like Mexico.

Ken Georgetti, president of the Canadian Labour Congress, and AFL-CIO president John Sweeney wrote to President Obama and Canadian Prime Minister [Stephen] Harper, reminding them that "the failure of neoliberal policies to create decent jobs in the Mexican economy under NAFTA has meant that many displaced workers and new entrants have been forced into a desperate search to find employment elsewhere." The new joint position of the AFL-CIO and Change to Win federations recognizes that "an essential component of the long-term solution is a fair trade and globalization model that uplifts all workers."

Continued support for work authorization and employer sanctions contradicts this understanding. Even with a legalization program, millions of people will remain without papers. For them, work without "authorization" will still be a crime. And while employer sanctions have little effect on migration, they will continue to make workers vulnerable to employer pressure.

When undocumented workers are fired for protesting low wages and bad conditions, employer sanctions bar them from receiving unemployment or disability benefits, although the workers have paid for them. It's much harder for them to find another job. An E-Verify database to deny them work will make this problem much worse.

The alternative to employer sanctions is enforcing the right to organize, minimum wage, overtime and other worker protection laws.

Workplace enforcement also increases discrimination. Four years after sanctions began, the Government Accountability Office reported that 346,000 U.S. employers applied immigration-verification requirements only to job applicants with a "foreign" accent or appearance. Another 430,000 [hired only] U.S.-born applicants.

Labor Rights Will Diminish for All

Despite these obstacles, immigrant workers, including the undocumented, have asserted their labor rights, organized unions and won better conditions. But employer sanctions have made this harder and riskier. When raids and document verification terrorized immigrants at Smithfield's huge packinghouse in Tar Heel, North Carolina, it became harder for black and white workers to organize as well. Using Social Security numbers to verify immigration status makes the firing and blacklisting of union activists all but inevitable. Citizens and permanent residents feel this impact because in our diverse workplaces, immigrant and native-born workers work together.

Low wages for undocumented workers will rise only if those workers can organize. The Employee Free Choice Act would make organizing easier for all workers. But "work authorization" will rob millions of immigrant workers of their ability to use the process that act would establish.

The alternative to employer sanctions is enforcing the right to organize, minimum wage, overtime and other worker protection laws. Eliminating sanctions will not change the requirement that people immigrate here legally. ICE will still have the power to enforce immigration law. And if a fair legalization program were passed at the same time sanctions were eliminated, many undocumented workers already here would normalize their status. A more generous policy for issuing residence and family-unification visas would allow families to cross the border legally, without the indentured servitude of guest-worker programs.

Immigrant rights plus jobs programs that require employers to hire from communities with high unemployment can reduce competition and fear. Together they would strengthen unions, raise incomes, contribute to the nation's economic recovery and bring the people of our country together. Employer sanctions will continue to tear us apart.

4

Immigration Raids Are Justified Because Lawbreakers Are Criminals

William P. Hoar

William P. Hoar is an author and magazine columnist. He is the author of Handouts and Pickpockets: Our Government Gone Berserk.

Despite some of the rhetoric to the contrary, law-abiding people of Hispanic background in America have nothing to fear from immigration agents. Illegal immigrants, residing in America against the law, are criminals and should be treated as such. In recent years the nation's immigration laws have not been adequately enforced, although there are some promising signs of attrition through enforcement when the laws have been enforced. The borders must be secured and existing immigration law must be enforced in order to eliminate the problem of illegal immigration, which brings along with it costs to society by draining public resources and increasing crime.

ITEM: The Associated Press [AP] reported on August 28, [2008]. "Hispanics should not have to live in fear of raids by immigration agents, Michelle Obama told a Hispanic caucus to the Democratic National Convention on Wednesday [August 27, 2008]. . . . 'We would have an immigration policy that brings 12 million people out of the shadows,' she told cheering caucus members who shouted 'Yes we can' in Spanish."

William P. Hoar, "Some Progress on the Illegal Immigration Front," *The New American*, vol. 24, September 29, 2008, pp. 42–43. Copyright © 2008 American Opinion Publishing Incorporated. Reproduced by permission.

ITEM: Federal officials, reported *The New York Times* on August 27, [2008], "revised upward to 595 the number of suspected illegal immigrants arrested this week in a raid on a Laurel, Miss., [electronics] factory, making it the largest immigration crackdown on a United States workplace in recent years."

ITEM: The AP, in an article headlined "Fear grips immigrants after Miss., plant raid," cited a youth pastor at Iglesia Cristiana Peniel, where up to 40 percent of the parishioners "were caught in the raid" at the factory in southern Mississippi. The youth pastor was quoted saying: "We have kids without dads and pregnant mothers who got their husbands taken away. It was like a horror story. They got handled like they were criminals."

Illegal Immigrants Are Criminals

CORRECTION: If you don't break the law, you have no reason to be afraid of immigration agents. Does the fear-mongering Michelle Obama really think that all American citizens with a Hispanic background are permanently terror-riven, unnerved that they will be rounded up and deported? Of course not. However, seeking more votes from those who support illegal aliens, she pretends that is the case.

Meanwhile, the above youth pastor—as well as the headline writer who typically left off the meaningful word "illegal" in front of "immigrants"—conveniently omitted the most pertinent fact: lawbreakers *are* criminals.

Moreover, about 100 of those detained were quickly released, according to the Justice Department [DOJ]. Many of these were mothers who were fitted with electronic monitoring devices and permitted to return home to their children. There's no doubt that having a parent arrested isn't the best thing to happen to a family, but law enforcement is bound to inconvenience those who flout the laws, whether those statutes have to do with stealing from a gas station or stealing someone's identity.

It is misleading to focus only on such people. Some of those arrested at the electronics-manufacturing company, as noted in *IT World*, "are being held on identity theft-related charges, the DOJ said. Investigators are looking into other charges, including the fraudulent use of Social Security numbers. . . . 'Identity theft is a growing problem in the United States, and the Department of Justice has prioritized bringing perpetrators of these crime to justice and protecting the interest of innocent victims,' Stan Harris, first assistant U.S. attorney for the Southern District of Mississippi, said in a statement." The Justice Department also noted that those arrested came from a number of foreign countries, including Germany, Peru, Mexico, El Salvador, Guatemala, Panama, Honduras, and Brazil.

Enforcement of Immigration Laws

The [George W.] Bush administration for years has been remarkably soft in enforcing the nation's immigrations laws. Recently, there seemed to be a bit of a shift, though it's hard not to be skeptical about ulterior motives. And the most recent administration enforcement program, dubbed Operation Scheduled Departure, seemed to be created for the express purpose of failing. *The New York Times*, for example, editorially mocked this strategy, which asked illegal to turn themselves in to the government.

Enforcing the law against hiring illegals, even though it happens very sporadically, does attract attention.

The *San Antonio Express-News* described the results as follows:

With eight down and 456.992 to go, immigration agents called it quits.

The Department of Homeland Security [DHS] on Friday [August 22, 2008] scrapped Operation Scheduled Departure, a program to encourage immigrants with deportation orders and no criminal records to come out of the shadows and self-deport.

U.S. Immigration and Customs Enforcement, the DHS agency managing the program, confirmed that eight people signed up in the 2 [frac12] weeks since it was rolled out Aug. 5 [2008]—out of 457,000 eligible candidates across the country and nearly 30,000 in five test cities.

Those in the country illegally do pay attention to events in Washington that could affect them. When the [George W.] Bush administration's amnesty program failed to make it through Congress earlier this year [2008], many illegals took notice and acted accordingly, including some who bought tickets to return to their native countries. Whether it was the intention of the administration or not, a certain amount of "attrition through enforcement" has been taking place, and estimated total number of illegal aliens in the United States appears to have started down.

Enforcing the law against hiring illegals, even though it happens very sporadically, does attract attention. A voluntary identity program called E-Verify is also currently available to employers. In short, there are ways to improve the situation without pretending that the only alternatives are deporting every illegal or legalizing all of them (the latter being, essentially, the position of both Barack Obama and John McCain [both presidential candidates at the time of this article]).

Attrition Through Enforcement

As it happens, Mexico is now getting a small taste of what has been happening in the United States for years. Mexicans are returning to Mexico, reports Fox News, "in numbers not seen for decades—and the Mexican government may have to deal with a crush on its social services and lower wages once the immigrants arrive." Large numbers of Mexican nationals are finding their way to the Mexican Consulate's office in Dallas

[Texas] to find out "what documentation they'll need to enroll their children in Mexican schools. 'Those numbers have increased percentage-wise tremendously,' said Enrique Hubbard, the Mexican consul general in Dallas. 'In fact, it's almost 100 percent more this year than it was the previous two years.'"

Mark Krikorian, executive director of the Center for Immigration Studies, is concerned that the next U.S. administration will toss overboard even limited enforcement efforts concerning illegal immigration. Writes Krikorian:

> Now there is research showing that attrition through enforcement works. A new report from the Center for Immigration Studies . . . used Census Bureau surveys to estimate that the illegal-immigrant population has fallen from a peak of 12.5 million in August of last year [2007] down to 11.2 million this past May [2008], a drop of 1.3 million or 11 percent. This decline is at least seven times larger than the number of people removed from the country by the immigration authorities during that period, meaning that most of the drop was due to illegal immigrants deporting themselves. If that rate of decrease were to continue, the illegal population would be cut in half in five years.
>
> So far, so good. But did enforcement contribute to the decline or was it driven just by the weakening economy? Though the slowdown in construction and other industries no doubt contributed to the decline, there are several reasons to think that enforcement was a major factor in the decision of illegal immigrants to leave. First of all, the decline in the number of illegal immigrants started before their unemployment rate increased; in the past, much smaller dips had been seen in the illegal population, but only after their unemployment rate increased—which stands to reason, of course. What's more, only the illegal population declined; the number of legal immigrants continued to grow.

Trends can be reversed quickly, in either direction. Illegal aliens respond to sanctions, both positive and negative, just as other people do. Should the borders be thrown open even further, millions more would also pour into the country.

The Cost of Illegal Immigrants

This is costing legal American taxpayers a huge amount of money, not to mention rending the nation's fabric. Up to $22 billion is being spent annually on the families of illegal immigrants by the various state governments, writes Jim Camp for Family Security Matters.

This includes $2.2 billion a year on assistance programs such as Food Stamps and free school lunches. An estimated $2.5 billion annually goes to Medicaid, says Camp. "The demands on some American hospitals have forced some to close emergency rooms as illegal immigrants crowd them and the law requires their care despite their inability to pay for it. Approximately $12 billion is spent on primary and secondary school education for children that are here illegally, many of whom cannot speak English." Then there is the $3 million daily "to incarcerate illegal aliens, and 30% of all federal prison inmates are illegal immigrants. The crime rates of illegal immigrants are estimated to be two-and-a-half times higher than native-born Americans for crimes that include illicit drugs, rape and murder."

The major candidates for president [in 2008], sadly, are ignoring these facts. This does make the job harder. But can we Americans actually control our own borders? ¡Sí, se puede! [Yes, we can!]

5

Immigration Raids Turn Victims into Criminals and Violate Worker Rights

Danielle Maestretti

Danielle Maestretti is librarian for the Utne Reader, *a digest of independent ideas and alternative culture.*

Recent raids at workplaces by immigration officials are a threat to workers' rights. The immigration raids spawn fear among undocumented workers and other members of the community. Within the current system of immigration enforcement, there is evidence of union busting by employers and racial profiling by local law enforcement. In addition, there is evidence of problems with the detention centers used to detain individuals for deportation proceedings, including a lack of adequate medical care and concerns about child welfare. The current problems point to a need for immigration reform.

More than 6,200 people were arrested for showing up to work [last year] in 2008, casualties of an unprecedented surge in raids by immigration officials. The workplace raids made big headlines, which dutifully announced staggering arrest counts in Postville, Iowa (389), Greenville, South Carolina (330), Laurel, Mississippi (592), and other cities and towns.

Raids and Workers' Rights

In the absence of meaningful immigration reform, we've arrived at a de facto policy that punishes workers, not the corporate bosses who benefit from their low wages and long

Danielle Maestretti, "Shelf Life: Immorally Detained," *Utne Reader*, January-February 2009, pp. 22–23. Reproduced by permission.

hours. Just 135 of last year's [2008's] 6,200 workplace arrests were owners, supervisors, or managers, according to the U.S. Immigration and Customs Enforcement (ICE) agency. What's more, a raid puts a community through the [wringer]: People are afraid to leave their homes to go to the grocery store or to their jobs. Children, some who are U.S. citizens, unknowingly sit through math class while their parents are hauled off to a remote detention center. Once-flourishing church congregations wilt and wither.

The raids are the most visible symptom of a dysfunctional system—and, perversely, the government may be stepping them up to push for the policies that corporate America wants. Writing for the *Nation*, David Bacon argues that the dramatic expansion of workplace raids is part of ICE's strategy to convince Congress to pass "an immigration reform package centered on guest-worker programs," which by nature tend to stifle workers' rights by limiting their ability to organize.

More deportations mean more detentions, and more jail cells.

In the meantime, ICE dabbles in its own brand of union busting. A *Washington Monthly* investigation found "disturbing evidence to suggest that unscrupulous employers are leaning heavily on ICE" to threaten undocumented workers involved in unionization drives or complaints about working conditions. *In These Times* notes that the Howard Industries electronics factory in Laurel, Mississippi, site of the largest workplace raid on record, "was in the midst of contentious union contract negotiations" when agents stormed in on August 25 [2008]. And a May [2008] raid on the Postville, Iowa Agriprocessors plant stopped a unionization drive dead in its tracks, reports *Labor Notes*. Just another example of the ICE acting as a "rogue agency," a union spokesman told the magazine.

Raids drum up plenty of fear among undocumented workers, their families, and their communities, and so does another much-criticized ICE initiative: the 287(g) program, which trains local police to "enforce immigration law." ICE likes to toot its crime-stopping horn, but in Arizona's Maricopa County, according to the *Phoenix New Times*, the 287(g) program basically boils down to racial profiling—"roundups of Mexicans and anybody who looks Mexican." People are being deported for minor crimes like driving without a license or a seat belt. In North Carolina, five men were arrested for fishing without licenses and later deported, reports the *Independent Weekly*.

Enforcement and Detention

ICE proudly claims that it deported 349,041 "illegal aliens" last year. That's 60,000 more people than the agency "removed" in 2007, an increase the *Washington Post* attributes in part to 287(g), which has "essentially transformed police, state troopers, deputies, and jail and prison guards into part-time immigration enforcers," the *Phoenix New Times* reports.

More deportations mean more detentions, and more jail cells: ICE "holds some 30,000 people on any given day," according to *Mother Jones*, and private prison corporations are only too happy to rent out their beds. *The Business of Detention*, an online investigative project by Renee Feltz and Stokely Baksh, documents ICE's contracts with bigwigs like the Corrections Corporation of America (CCA), where business is booming. ICE pays the company significantly more—in some cases, $200 a day per detainee—than the $54 or so CCA normally charges to house federal or state prisoners.

The *Washington Post* has done excellent front-page reporting on the abominable medical care provided by (or, more frequently, withheld from) these often private-run immigrant detention centers. For the newspaper's four-part series "Careless Detention," Dana Priest and Amy Goldstein investigated cases in which detainees died in custody or shortly thereafter—83 in the past five years [2004–2008]—and found repeated instances of "medical neglect." *Seattle Weekly* reports that it took Juan Carlos Martinez-Mendez, who is detained at the Northwest Detention Center in Tacoma [Washington], two years to get the surgery necessary to repair his "potentially life-threatening" sinus infections—even after repeated interventions from his regular doctor, a boost of support most detainees don't have.

Immigration and Child Welfare

All of this probably doesn't trouble the Lou Dobbs [anti-illegal immigration] crowd. But here's a question that might get through to those folks: What about the children?

So far, it seems, there isn't much of a system in place for them. Some kids get locked up with their parents at one of the country's two "residential" facilities that house families. One of them, the CCA-run T. Don Hutto Center in Taylor, Texas, was forced to improve conditions after being sued by the American Civil Liberties Union in 2007. Since then, the *San Antonio Current* reports, razor wire has been removed, more educational programs have been introduced, and food has gotten more nutritious—but it's still just a big prison, a renovated medium-security facility filled with parents and children awaiting deportation. And it costs ICE $2.8 million a month.

It's difficult to advocate for those children, writes Melissa del Bosque for the *Texas Observer*, because federal and state agencies clash over whose turf it is. "Child welfare is a state issue," she notes, while "immigration is a federal issue."

Right now, the issue—all the issues—seems to belong to ICE. Writing on *Truthout.org*, David Bacon calls for an end to workplace raids and community sweeps within the much-hyped first hundred days of Barack Obama's presidency.

"Something is clearly wrong with the priorities of immigration enforcement," he writes. "Hungry and desperate workers go to jail and get deported."

Scores of passionate writers and activists are working to put immigration reform back on the agenda. I like to direct people to New America Media, whose editors have equipped immigrants in the post-raid community of Postville, Iowa, with video cameras. One woman shows her black, bulky ankle monitoring device, which hovers above a hot-pink Croc. "I know that coming here and trying to find a better life for my family is not a crime," she says.

6

Immigration Raids Justify Counter Exploitation of Illegal Immigrants

Jamie Glazov

Jamie Glazov is an editor at FrontPage Magazine. Here she interviews Stephen Steinlight, a senior policy analyst at the Center for Immigration Studies, a think tank that analyzes the economic, social, demographic, fiscal, and other impacts of immigration on the United States.

The current massive immigration to the United States by poor and uneducated immigrants leads to their exploitation. Despite what liberal members of the left wing claim, it is the poverty of illegal immigrants that leads to exploitation, not their legal status. As such, opening the borders or providing amnesty will not remedy the fact that employers will exploit these immigrants. Rather than toning down immigration enforcement, enforcement should be stepped up, as recent increases in enforcement have resulted in the desirable attrition of illegal immigrants. This exploitation that occurs under the current immigration policy not only harms illegal immigrants, but also ends up victimizing American workers.

FrontPage Magazine: Last May, 2008, the U.S. Immigration and Customs Enforcement agency (ICE) raided the AgriProcessors meat processing plant in Postville, Iowa. Tell us what it was about exactly.

Stephen Steinlight: Until an even bigger raid last month [August 2008], the raid at the AgriProcessors meat processing plant briefly held the dubious distinction of being the largest immigration workplace enforcement action in US history, with 389 arrests of illegal aliens. Like several other large-scale ICE raids, the action in Iowa uncovered grotesque exploitation of illegal workers.

Immigration and Exploitation

The significance?

Most significant about the Iowa raid is that it has culminated in criminal charges against the owners and managers of the plant, and not solely against their miserable helots [slaves]. The attorney general of the state of Iowa has indicted the company, its owners and managers on 9,311 counts of violating state laws against child labor as well as conspiring in hiring illegal aliens, including providing them forged green cards and other false documentation. Such scurrilous employers are the magnets and enablers that bring illegal labor to this country and have infinitely more moral agency than their workers. The attorney general's action is an all-too-rare example of justice and sound social policy.

What did the raid demonstrate?

The raid demonstrates that massive immigration by the uneducated, unskilled and impoverished to a knowledge-based, largely post-industrial America is joined at the hip to exploitation. If one supports massive immigration—currently at the highest level in all of American history with the immigrants, legal and illegal, comprised predominantly of unskilled, uneducated and impoverished Hispanics—one must be prepared to countenance their exploitation and be complicit, knowingly or unwittingly, in permitting whole sectors of corporate America to return to the moral universe of unfettered capitalism portrayed in Upton Sinclair's [novel] *The Jungle*. Neither wholesale violation of the rule of law by illegal aliens nor their brutal exploitation ought to be matters that divide the Left from the Right in America.

Open-Borders Proponents

What was the lib-Left's [liberal left wing] response to the raid? What did that response reflect?

Predictably, it was righteously indignant but uninformed, "post-American" in its indifference to the well-being of the nation and its citizens, selective in its moral outrage and repugnant in its attack on law enforcement. As a matter of "policy," the lib-Left's sole recommendation is legalizing the arrested illegal workers, part of their larger campaign for amnesty for all illegal aliens in America and passage of the legislation that would grant it as well as double legal immigration: "comprehensive immigration reform."

Every prescription from the lib-Lefts's open-borders camp (and let us be honest: it has many prominent conservative fellow travelers, among them [Senator] John McCain, [President of Americans for Tax Reform] Grover Norquist and most libertarians) is a variant on the mantra about "bringing them out of the shadows." Policy-savvy advocates recognize it's a sham solution and mouth the slogan to pander to Hispanic voters while rewarding cronies with cheap labor. They know the poverty that causes illegal aliens to work for ruthless exploiters is the product of their lack of education, not legal status. Fully 62% of Mexicans and Central Americans who reside in the US lack a high school diploma: that's true of only 8% of American workers.

Hard evidence confirms robust enforcement works.

Perhaps worst of all, the open-borders camp has also determined to make a new PR [public relations] strategy of vilifying ICE agents; even some members of Congress have engaged in the morally disgusting act of equating ICE agents with the Gestapo [Nazi Germany's secret police].

A Policy of Attrition

What did the raid say about the more muscular immigration enforcement we've been witnessing within the last year?

Whatever the [George W. Bush] administration's genuine motivations, there has been far more robust internal enforcement of immigration law in the past year [2007–2008] than in all [of] George [W.] Bush's presidency [preceding it]. This takes the form of large-scale ICE raids; amending or abandoning statutes hindering cooperation between local police and federal immigration agents in many jurisdictions; and the hundreds of ordinances—designed to see the lives of illegal aliens are not regularized and [to] promote their [illegals'] removal—adopted by states, counties and municipalities after immigration policy effectively devolved upon them in the wake of the June 28, 2007, defeat of S.1639 [The Bush-Kennedy Amnesty Bill], the latest incarnation of "comprehensive immigration reform."

Hard evidence confirms robust enforcement works. An important recent study by my think tank, the Center for Immigration Studies, titled "Homeward Bound: Recent Immigration Enforcement and the Decline in the Illegal Alien Population," provides a wealth of data supporting this claim. After peaking in August 2007, the illegal population has fallen from 12.5 million to 11.2 million, or 11%, through May of 2008. The decline—a product of self-deportation from an increasingly inhospitable environment—exceeds by a factor of 7 the number of illegal aliens deported by the government. While the downturn in the economy, particularly in construction, accounts for a fraction of the departures, significant self-removal began before the onset of the current recession. Over the same period, legal immigration has remained constant. It's also worth noting that the decline began shortly after the defeat of S.1639, a bill whose victory was widely anticipated and whose progress was closely followed in the immigrant and immigrant-advocacy community. The report concludes that if the present decline were to continue, the illegal population would be cut in half within the next five years.

The mass of uneducated and unskilled immigrant workers is lowering wages and worsening working conditions for millions of Americans.

Such a policy of "attrition" is favored by an overwhelming majority of Americans every time it is offered as an option in public opinion surveys. The only occasions when a majority of Americans indicate support for "a path to citizenship" for illegal aliens is in push polls that offer only two alternatives: amnesty, which most Americans abhor, or wholesale deportation, which conjures images of boxcars headed for Auschwitz. But whenever a third choice is available to respondents in public opinion polls—as is the case in surveys by Rasmussen and Zogby—of incremental removal of the illegal population through strong border enforcement and vigorous internal enforcement of immigration law, between 67%–79% of respondents select it over amnesty. Though every conceivable effort has been made to exclude the American people from participating in the debate on immigration or to disinform them with regard to it, their good sense prevails.

The Victims of Mass Immigration

Who are the real victims of mass immigration?

I'm grateful you have used the phrase "victims of mass immigration," because this transformational social engineering has produced and is producing millions of victims. The mass immigration we're experiencing by the uneducated and unskilled is having a disastrous impact on the most vulnerable of our fellow citizens: the unemployed, partially employed, the elderly still working, African American males, recent legal immigrants, young people entering the job market, and all working-class or lower-middle class Americans with no more than a high school education. These consequences are not debatable: a wealth of data from the most prestigious social science research bodies has established them as fact. Among the most significant literature is the National Research Council of the American Academy of Science's study *New Americans: Economic, Demographic and Fiscal Effects of Immigrants*; the National Bureau of Economic Research's *Immigration and African-American Employment*; and the Russell Sage and Ford Foundation's *Multi-City Study of Urban Inequality*, among other seminal work. The mass of uneducated and unskilled immigrant workers is lowering wages and worsening working conditions for millions of Americans while creating feverish competition for the shrinking stock of low-income urban housing, with resultant social conflict, most often, between black and brown.

7

Illegal Immigrants Should Not Be Allowed Amnesty

Christopher M. Jaarda

Christopher M. Jaarda is director of government relations for the Federation for American Immigration Reform (FAIR), an organization that seeks to improve border security, to stop illegal immigration, and to promote immigration levels consistent with the national interest.

Amnesty for illegal aliens is currently under consideration as part of comprehensive immigration reform legislation. Granting amnesty to immigrants currently in the United States illegally is a bad idea given the historically high unemployment at the moment. It's hard to see why Congress would consider amnesty now, given that such amnesty was rejected in 2007, when unemployment was not nearly as bad as it is now. Especially given the current employment statistics, the argument that immigrants or guest workers do jobs that Americans do not want falls completely flat. Americans need jobs, and amnesty for illegal aliens should be rejected.

With an official unemployment rate of 9.5 percent, American workers now face the worst job market in 25 years. In fact, over the past 60 years, the unemployment rate has rarely been as high as it is today [June 2009]. Despite a difficult job market, President [Barack] Obama and leaders in Congress are talking about passing so-called "comprehensive

Christopher M. Jaarda, "Introduction; Conclusion," *Amnesty and Joblessness: 14.7 Million Unemployed Americans Shouldn't Have to Compete for Jobs with Today's Illegal Aliens.* June 2009, pp. 2–6. Reproduced by permission.

immigration reform" legislation. This legislation would give amnesty to 12 million or more illegal aliens, including an esti- mated 8.3 million illegal aliens who hold jobs they never should have had, and could include a proposed new guest- worker provision to import hundreds of thousands of addi- tional foreign workers. If enacted, illegal aliens would be al- lowed to keep these jobs instead of making them available to American citizens and legal immigrants who are out of work. Congress has a responsibility to ensure that the law that re- quires available jobs to be filled by legal workers is respected. Consideration of amnesty, particularly in these harsh eco- nomic times, constitutes a failure by Congress to live up to its basic responsibilities to the American people.

Historically High Unemployment

American workers are struggling. The number of available jobs continues to shrink. Today [June 2009], 14.7 million Americans are out of work and looking for a job, and millions more are in temporary part-time jobs while they look for per- manent jobs. At the same time, it is estimated that 8.3 million illegal aliens are part of the American workforce despite not being legally authorized to work in the United States. Earlier this month [June 2009], the Bureau of Labor Statistics (BLS) reported that 467,000 jobs were lost in the month of June alone. In just the past year [2008–2009], 5.8 million jobs have been lost.

For months, leaders in Congress have been telling the American people that the U.S. economy is facing significant challenges. For example, during debate on President Obama's $800 billion stimulus bill, Senator Charles Schumer (D-N.Y.) said that "The country is in tough shape. We have had the most difficult economic time since the Great Depression." Since he made that remark in February [2009], the economy and the job situation has continued its downward spiral. While today's official 9.5 percent unemployment rate is nowhere near as bad as the 24.8 percent seen in 1933, during the depths of the Great Depression, the current unemployment rate is the highest Americans have seen in the past 25 years. . . .

It is surprising that Congress would even consider amnesty [for illegal aliens] given the current economic climate.

Put in historic perspective, today's workers are facing an unemployment rate that has rarely been seen since World War II. The job market presents significant challenges for those Americans who are out of work and looking for a job.

Reform with Amnesty

Despite the jobless picture, Senator Schumer, who recently compared today's economy to that of the Great Depression, recently chaired a hearing entitled "Comprehensive Immigration Reform in 2009, Can We Do It and How?" The hearing was held on April 30, 2009, before the Senate Judiciary Committee, Subcommittee on Immigration, Border Security and Refugees. Critics say that so-called "comprehensive" reform is a euphemism for legislation that would grant amnesty to 12 million illegal aliens and that this hearing is the first step towards consideration of amnesty in the 111th Congress.

While it comes as no surprise that Schumer would push amnesty, since he has supported it in the past, it is surprising that Congress would even consider amnesty given the current economic climate. Even people from Schumer's own state of New York recognize the reality that pushing amnesty with today's job market is unwise. For example, Rogan Kersh, a dean at New York University's Wagner [Graduate] School of Public Service, has stated that "rising unemployment rates, coupled with continuing dismal economic news, are battering the public's inclination to back a change in illegal immigrants' status, which was never that strong to begin with."

Underlying Dean Kersh's comment is the fact that the American people intuitively understand that amnesty legislation would authorize illegal aliens to stay in the United States and allow them to keep jobs they should never have had in the first place. The American people understand that, rather than granting amnesty, Congress and the [Obama] administration should focus on immigration enforcement, which would progressively make available to legal American workers those jobs currently held by illegal aliens. Despite the lack of available jobs for legal American workers and the support of the American people for immigration law enforcement, Senator Schumer has said he will be undeterred by "difficult economic conditions" and will press ahead with the hearing, noting that there is "a real chance of passing comprehensive reform this year [2009]."

The Last Amnesty Debate

When Congress last considered amnesty in May and June 2007, some politicians suggested that illegal aliens were doing jobs that no Americans would do. That was not true then, and it certainly is not true today [June 2009]. Representative Steve King (R-Iowa) has made just that point, saying that amnesty supporters "are going to have to be faced with the argument that I and many others are making: Illegals are taking jobs Americans now want." Amnesty would allow an estimated 8.3 million illegal aliens to keep the jobs they currently hold, even though they never should have been hired for those jobs in the first place. In addition, amnesty would allow anyone who is illegally present in the United States to openly begin applying for any and every available job in America. This would put American workers in the position of having to openly compete with (former) illegal aliens to fill an available job. American workers shouldn't have to do that, but amnesty would force them to.

The last time Congress rejected amnesty, in May and June 2007, America's economy was in much better shape than it is today. At that time, big business interests supported amnesty and President [George W.] Bush's guest-worker program, which would have brought in hundreds of thousands of guest-workers each year. If the job market could not support those policies in 2007, there is no doubt that the current lack of available American jobs means that America simply cannot support these policies today. . . .

Real enforcement and a reduction in immigration levels would ensure that America restores the integrity of its labor market.

During the 2007 amnesty debate, official unemployment (seasonal) stood at 4.6 percent—4.9 full points lower than the current 9.5 percent. It also shows that in June 2007, nearly 7.0 million Americans were out of work, compared to 14.7 million today. In June 2009, 7.7 million more Americans are out of work and actively looking for a job than were in 2007. In June 2007, the Bureau of Labor Statistics [BLS] reported that America lost 184,000 jobs in the month of May 2007. By comparison, BLS reported that in June 2009, America had lost 467,000 jobs over the previous month.

During the last amnesty debate, the number of unemployed Americans declined by 139,000 during the year prior to the debate (comparing July 2006 to June 2007). Over that same one-year period, the unemployment rate had declined slightly from 4.7 to 4.6 percent. By comparison, America has had a net loss of nearly 5.8 million jobs during the previous one-year period (July 2008 to June 2009) and unemployment has increased by 3.7 percentage points. These numbers translate to a significantly higher number of Americans who are out of work today than were in 2007 (7.7 million more Americans) and suggests that America simply does not need more foreign workers, whether through amnesty, legalization or a guest-worker program. In fact, real enforcement and a reduction in immigration levels would ensure that America restores the integrity of its labor market, which would increase wages and free jobs for American workers. . . .

Unemployment in America Today

Regardless of race or national origin, Americans across the board are living with employment prospects today [June 2009] that are much worse than in 2007. According to BLS, white unemployment is up 4.6 percentage points (from 4.1 to 8.7 percent), Hispanic unemployment is up 6.6 percentage points (from 5.6 to 12.2 percent), and unemployment for African-Americans is up 6.2 percentage points (from 8.5 to 14.7 percent). Immigrant unemployment—mostly legal workers—in the first quarter of 2009 was even higher, i.e., 9.7 percent—the highest level since 1994, when data began to be collected for immigrants. Similarly, the teenage unemployment rate, having risen from 16.1 percent in June 2007 to 24.0 percent in June 2009, is also considerably higher. The teenage unemployment rate for African-Americans, at 37.9 percent, is even higher than the national average for all teenagers.

As with other demographics, job losses have hit Americans hard regardless of their level of educational attainment. According to BLS, workers over the age of 25 who have earned a college degree or higher have seen their unemployment rate more than double from 2.0 percent in June 2007 to 4.4 percent in June 2009. The unemployment rate for people with some college but without a degree has more than doubled from 3.6 percent to 8.0 percent, from June 2007 to June 2009.

The hardest hit, however, are those Americans older than 25 with "less than a high school diploma." These Americans have seen their demographic's unemployment climb from 6.8 percent to 15.5 percent, from June 2007 to June 2009. Those with a high school diploma but no college have seen unemployment increase from 4.2 percent to 9.8 percent. These numbers represent 1.9 million unemployed Americans without a high school diploma, and 3.8 million more with a high school diploma but no college.

Competition for Jobs

According to the Pew Hispanic Center, illegal aliens are "especially likely to hold low-skilled jobs" because they are "disproportionately likely to be poorly educated." According to the Pew research, nearly half of all illegal aliens (47 percent) ages 25 to 64 have "less than a high school education," compared to 8 percent of U.S.-born residents in that age group who have not graduated from high school. Americans who dropped out of high school or completed high school but never attended college will necessarily have to compete in the job market with any illegal alien who receives amnesty and anyone admitted under a new "no skill/low skill" "guest-worker program." Americans with no more than a high school diploma, including 5.7 million Americans who are currently unemployed, are the most likely to be economically disadvantaged and are also most likely to be the hardest hit by amnesty or by a guest-worker program.

America's unemployment numbers, taken as a whole, demonstrate an alarming trend for American workers. Unemployment is much higher today [June 2009]—across all demographics and regardless of gender, race, age or education level—than it was the last time Congress considered amnesty in June 2007. Amnesty would force those Americans out of work and looking for a job to compete with today's illegal aliens for the limited number of jobs. The jobless numbers suggest that American workers cannot afford a guest-worker program and that American taxpayers cannot afford amnesty for millions of illegal aliens who would then become eligible for unemployment benefits. Despite this reality for the American worker, Congress has begun holding hearings on amnesty.

But the conclusion is unavoidable: if consideration of amnesty was "ripe" in 2007, by today's standards it is simply "rotten."

8

Ethical Considerations Support Amnesty for Illegal Immigrants

David DeCosse

David DeCosse is the director of campus ethics programs at the Markkula Center for Applied Ethics at Santa Clara University in California.

There are three key ethical considerations that support some kind of earned citizenship, or amnesty, for illegal immigrants. First, most serious amnesty proposals do not simply allow illegal immigrants to become citizens; such proposals also involve a penalty for being undocumented in the past and a lengthy process to become a citizen. Second, the common humanity of illegal immigrants should be taken into account by understanding that illegal immigrants come here seeking a better life. Third, it is important to uphold the law, but allowing a path to earned citizenship is compatible with this, punishing illegal immigrants according to intent and effect.

"Amnesty": Just include this lightning rod of a word and any proposal for legalizing undocumented immigrants or for achieving comprehensive immigration reform quickly plummets to defeat. Yet that need not be the case. In order to clarify use of the term amnesty in the national debate, I offer three ethical considerations that every policy maker and in-

David DeCosse, "Can Citizenship Be Earned?" *America*, vol. 199, October 13, 2008, pp. 10–12. Copyright © 2008 www.americamagazine.org. All rights reserved. Reproduced by permission of America Press. For subscription information, visit www.americamagazine .org.

formed voter ought to keep in mind this fall [2008 presidential election]. These points emerged during intensive discussion among a group of immigration experts (ethicists, lawyers, scholars and policy makers) who were convened recently by the Markkula Center for Applied Ethics at Santa Clara University.

The Meaning of Amnesty

How one understands the legal meaning of amnesty makes a difference. But how one understands the ethical values at stake in the immigration debate matters even more.

1. The use of the word amnesty is almost always an exaggeration, if not outright dishonest.

Technically, amnesty means the lifting of a penalty associated with an entire class of people who have violated a law. But every serious legalization proposal includes a stiff penalty for immigrants without documents, and thus none is in fact an amnesty. One proposal, for instance, would confer permanent residency only after all of the following criteria are met: eight years of employment in the United States, payment of a substantial fine and any back taxes owed, learning the English language and getting in line behind all those who have already applied for lawful residence. By one estimate, it would take an undocumented immigrant 11 to 13 years to become a U.S. citizen under this proposal. The current legislative proposals for what has been called "earned citizenship" are not like the 1986 immigration legislation, which extended permanent residency to the undocumented after only 18 months of residency and on the basis of a much less onerous work requirement.

Our Common Humanity

2. An ethically acceptable approach to the immigration debate must recognize the good faith and common humanity of persons without documents.

Where one stands in the debate over immigration policy depends greatly on how one views the motives of undocumented immigrants, the men and women who are working all across the country in places ranging from slaughterhouses and restaurants to expensive suburban homes. To those who take an enforcement-only approach, such immigrants are lawbreakers, period. From this view there is only a short series of steps to the assumption that such men and women also are inclined to criminality or to leeching off the U.S. welfare system or are in league with terrorists.

But one could view these immigrants more broadly and accurately, not only in terms of a legal violation but also in terms of the fundamental motives of a shared humanity. Then one could ask, to borrow a phrase about migrants from the French philosopher Simone Weil: Are not these men and women "exactly like us"? In asking this question, it becomes possible to see undocumented immigrants as more than violators of a law and deserving of deportation. Instead they emerge as fellow human beings, who have sometimes endured great hardship to seek a better life here, much as our ancestors did. One can see them as possessing inalienable human rights. One can see them as members of families: families in Mexico on whose behalf the undocumented immigrant risks much to cross the desert, and families in the United States that are broken whenever one member is deported. One can compare these immigrant stories with the stories of our own immigrant parents, grandparents and great-grandparents.

The legal dimension does not exhaust the narrative. It is not that the undocumented today came illegally, while all of our ancestors came legally. During past periods of heavy immigration to the United States, there was nothing like the legal regimen that governs immigration today. The common factor between then and now, between Ellis Island and today's slaughterhouses and suburbs, is the immigrants' brave hunger for a better life.

At the origins of Western civilization, the Hebrew Scriptures commanded, "You shall treat the alien who resides with you no differently than the natives born among you; have the same love for him as for yourself; for you too were once aliens in the land of Egypt." By seeing undocumented immigrants only as lawbreakers and as utterly unlike our law-abiding selves, we make it difficult to recognize the common hopes of our shared humanity.

It is important to recognize the social utility of the work undertaken by undocumented persons.

The Rule of Law

3. It is ethically legitimate, even desirable, to uphold the rule of law; the proposals for earned citizenship do this.

It is necessary to address the argument that any legalization proposal amounts to a de facto amnesty, because the person who has entered the United States without permission is able, through legalization, to reap the rewards of his or her legal violation and remain in this country. This is not an amnesty in the sense that a penalty is lifted, but it is one in the sense that no penalty is applied. For those who think this way, the fines imposed in the earned citizenship proposals are not punishment enough, because the immigrants would ultimately be allowed to remain in the United States. In this view, their retention of the fruit of an immigration violation—staying here—undermines the rule of law.

Amnesty and the rule of law, however, must be considered in light of how legal punishment is often determined. Two factors are especially crucial: the intent of the violator and the effect of the violator's action. By specifying these factors, punishment can be made to fit the offense. It is important to recognize the central intent of those who illegally cross the U.S. border: to seek a better life. Many come from conditions of crushing poverty. Determining the just punishment of a whole class of people who have violated a law by aspiring to a better life is a very different action from determining the punishment for a lawbreaker who crosses the border maliciously as the first step in a lawless sojourn in the United States. This is intent.

What about "effect"? It is important to recognize the social utility of the work undertaken by undocumented persons. This work needs to be done: picking crops, caring for children, constructing homes and maintaining lawns. The spiking demand for agricultural workers by growers across the United States who are squeezed by the enforcement-only strategy is powerful evidence of such need, as is the number of related proposals for expanded visa or guest-worker programs.

At the root of the rejection of what has been called amnesty lies a series of misguided ethical choices.

To make the punishment fit the violation in the case of the undocumented requires judgments about intent and effect. An abstract justice detached from concerns about circumstances and economic purpose would uphold the rule of law by deporting millions of undocumented men and women. But a justice attentive to the actual conditions of people's lives and to economic need would link the rule of law to the requirement that law itself should be subordinate to reality. Fairness requires that the punishment fit the offense. In other words, a substantial fine as part of earned citizenship proposals upholds the rule of law far better than does the unrealistic resort to deportation. It may also be the case that the law itself should be changed to conform to the new economic reality. As the legal maxim says: "When the reason for the rule ceases, so should the rule."

Resistance to Amnesty

Why has the word amnesty been wrenched from its full meaning and used to stifle reasonable efforts at legalization? One explanation is that many Americans think the undocumented are playing outside the rules by which fairness is established. Those who think this way may not be persuaded by blameless motives or even by the impossibility of deporting 12 million people. Another explanation is that proposals for earned citizenship are not well known throughout the country. One hopes that the more American citizens know about the penalties attached to the proposals, the more they will support them. Another possibility is that Americans are at a low point in their confidence in government: even if earned citizenship imposes a set of requirements on the undocumented, Americans have little hope that a government that cannot hold the borders could enforce such requirements on the immigrants who have already crossed them. And some detect the presence of a resurgent nativism in the U.S. population, fueled by suspicion of immigrants in the wake of the terrorist attacks on September 11, 2001.

At the root of the rejection of what has been called amnesty lies a series of misguided ethical choices. I hope this statement helps identify those choices and shows that it is possible to find just and ethical ways to deal with the legalization of the undocumented, ways that respect our shared humanity, acknowledge economic reality and uphold the rule of law.

9

Earned Legalization Is Preferable to Enforcement by Deportation

Patricia Hatch and Katherine Fennelly

Patricia Hatch and Katherine Fennelly are members of the League of Women Voters of the United States (LWVUS) Immigration Study Committee.

Unauthorized, or illegal, immigrants come to the United States for a variety of reasons, and many have been here for years. Using mass deportations as a method of dealing with unauthorized immigrants is a poor strategy. Such a method is costly, ties up the courts, and causes family and community disruption. A far better strategy to pursue is that of earned legalization, whereby unauthorized immigrants can register with the government for the chance at permanent residency and citizenship. Native-born Americans benefit from a strategy of earned legalization in many ways, including by freeing up resources and increasing the health of communities.

This essay highlights reasons why creating a pathway to legal status for unauthorized immigrants already in the U.S. would be preferable to [their mass deportation, both for the immigrant families and for] their U.S. citizen neighbors.

One of the most controversial issues in ongoing immigration discussions is the proposal to provide a path to legal residence for unauthorized immigrants currently residing in the

Patricia Hatch and Katherine Fennelly, "Unauthorized Immigrants: The Case for Earned Legalization," *National Voter*, vol. 57, June 2008, pp. 10–12. Reproduced by permission.

U.S. It has been a stumbling block in congressional efforts to pass comprehensive immigration reform legislation, and a barometer by which many voters are judging candidates for elected office. As a result of the LWVUS [League of Women Voters of the United States] Immigration Study, the League supports a path to earned legalization as part of comprehensive immigration reform.

---

3 million U.S. citizen children have at least one parent without legal residency.

Who Are Unauthorized Immigrants?

In 2006, there were an estimated 11.5 [million] to 12 million unauthorized immigrants in the U.S. Of this number, between 25 [percent] and 40 percent entered the U.S. legally but overstayed their visas. Many others entered the U.S. without authorization, to join U.S. citizen or legal permanent resident (LPR) family members after years of waiting "in line" for visas that never materialized.[1]

Many persons have entered the U.S. without authorization as an unintended consequence of the effects of international trade policies and globalization on their homelands.[2] Although the Bureau of Labor Statistics estimates that there will be 56 million new jobs created during the years 2002–12, and that 75 million baby-boomers will be retiring during the same period, our current, broken system does not provide a reasonably timely means of legal immigration for foreign workers who are willing and able to fill those positions. "Pulled" by the availability of jobs in the U.S. at wages that greatly surpass any they could hope for in their homelands, many have risked apprehension, detention and death to enter the U.S.[3]

Many unauthorized immigrants have lived in the U.S. for years and are virtually indistinguishable from naturalized citizens or LPRs residing in the same communities. The Urban

Institute estimates that at least 5 million children—including 3 million U.S. citizen children—have at least one parent without legal residency.[4]

What we, as a nation, choose to do about unauthorized immigrants currently in the U.S. will have far-reaching effects on their LPR and U.S. citizen family members, the businesses that employ them, and the economic and social health of the communities in which many have deep roots.

Feasibility of Mass Deportations

How feasible are mass deportations? In 2006, in a major push utilizing all the staff and resources at its disposal, Immigration and Customs Enforcement (ICE) was able to deport approximately 190,000 people. In September 2007, ICE Director Julie Myers estimated that to detain and remove 12 million people would cost at least $94 billion, more than twice the entire Department of Homeland Security 2008 budget, and nearly 18 times the current ICE budget.[5]

According to an ICE spokesperson, that figure does not include the cost of *locating* the illegal immigrants—arguably the most labor intensive and expensive part of such an operation—or the cost of immigration court hearings, where tremendous backlogs would create the need for much longer and significantly more costly detentions than the 30-day average cited in the ICE estimate.[6] One year after the much-publicized New Bedford [Massachusetts factory raid on March 6, 2007], 161 of the 361 immigrant workers initially taken into custody remain in U.S. detention facilities, awaiting the final adjudication of their cases.[7]

If mass deportations were attempted, what might be the effects on American communities? Recent ICE raids in targeted locations provide a small taste of the scale of family and community disruption likely to ensue if an attempt were made to deport 12 million residents from the U.S. It is estimated that for every two adults deported after the recent raids, one child was left behind, the majority under the age of five.[8]

In addition to the emotional impacts resulting from the abrupt separation of children from their parents in "mixed status" families, some communities where raids have taken place report abandoned housing, business closings due to lack of workers and dwindling customers, and dramatic drops in school attendance. Those unauthorized immigrants not caught in the first "wave" of deportations are likely to move deeper into the shadows of American society and become less productive and less invested in their communities.

For several weeks in 2000, the attention of the entire nation was focused on the plight of one child, Elian Gonzalez, who was forcibly returned to Cuba. That action sparked debate about the values reflected in our immigration policies. Deportations on a massive scale, with vivid images on the nightly news of parents being forcibly removed from their children and their homes, would shake many U.S. communities to their core.

Allowing Unauthorized Immigrants to Earn Legal Status

During the LWVUS Immigration Study Consensus process, local Leagues supported allowing unauthorized immigrants to earn legal status as an important element of any plan to restore law and order to our broken immigration system. How might such a policy work, and what effects might it have?

The McCain-Kennedy compromise immigration reform bill that failed to pass the Senate in 2007 would have provided a system through which unauthorized immigrants would pay to register with the government, go through rigorous background checks and security clearances, learn English and civics, pay any back taxes, work steadily for a number of years, and only then earn the right to go to the back of the line to wait for visas to remain in the U.S. legally and permanently.

Under that system, it would take at least a decade for the first unauthorized immigrants to earn the right to become legal permanent residents, and then five more years before they would be eligible to apply for citizenship. This complex and lengthy process has been mislabeled "amnesty" by some critics.

The Benefits of a Legalization Policy

The benefits of an orderly earned legalization policy to unauthorized immigrants are clear. They would obtain permission to work legally. Mixed status families could remain intact and could participate fully in their communities without fear and plan for the future with more confidence.

The likely benefits to native-born Americans are equally significant.

- As unauthorized immigrants submit to background checks, Homeland Security officers would be able to focus resources on pursuing criminal aliens, rather than those who are gainfully employed.

- Public safety would improve when newly legal residents no longer fear reporting crime to the police.

- Wages and working conditions would be likely to improve for all entry-level workers when abusive employers who have exploited the vulnerability of unauthorized workers are forced to compete with businesses that adhere to wage and labor standards.

- More Social Security taxes and income taxes would be paid to the federal and state governments by newly legalized workers, boosting the economy and helping to stabilize Social Security and Medicare.

- Public health would be likely to improve when newly legal residents can seek preventive care, rather than delaying treatment for illnesses.

- Immigrants who learn English and civics would be more likely to assimilate and become more fully invested in their communities.

- As the federal government restores order and sanity to the immigration system, state and local governments would be able to spend their tax dollars on services that benefit all their constituents, rather than trying to enforce federal immigration laws.

The Future

The future of immigration reform in the U.S. is unclear. However, what has been sorely missing from the debates is a discussion of the *values* that should underpin our immigration policy. Once the smoke of campaign rhetoric clears, there may be an opportunity for more rational discussions of how to achieve realistic comprehensive reform that promotes economic goals, humanitarian objectives and national security. The League is poised to contribute to a solution.

Notes

1. "Family Reunification" LWVUS Immigration Study (IS) paper at www.lwv.org.
2. "Effects of Global Interdependence on Migration" IS paper at www.lwv.org.
3. "Economic Aspects of Authorized and Unauthorized Immigration," "Immigration and the Economy," "What Motivates Immigration to America?" IS papers at www.lwv.org.
4. Capps, Randy, "Paying the Price: The Effect of Immigration Raids on America's Children," Urban Institute and NCLR, 2007.
5. http://www.dhs.gov/xabout/budget.
6. www.cnn.com/2007/U.S./09/12/deportation.cost/incdex.html.
7. "A Year After Raid, Immigration Cases Drag On," *Boston Globe*, March 6, 2008.
8. Capps, "Paying the Price."

Illegal Alien Criminals Should Be Removed from the Country

Jessica Vaughan and James R. Edwards, Jr.

Jessica Vaughan is director of policy studies at the Center for Immigration Studies, and James R. Edwards, Jr. is coauthor of The Congressional Politics of Immigration Reform.

There are many concerns about crime caused by illegal aliens and, in the past, it has been challenging for the federal government to address the problem on its own. A program known as 287(g) pays for local law enforcement to help in the effort. The program is geared toward locally identifying, incarcerating, and deporting criminals who are illegal immigrants. The program has worked well to decrease the number of illegal immigrant criminals in the country, and there is a high demand for it. Congress needs to work to ensure that this program is not ended, in spite of its hysterical critics.

With the widespread murderous violence between warring Mexican drug cartels spilling over the U.S. border and the continuing threat from radical Islamic terrorists domestic and foreign, the government has to spend its law enforcement dollars where they can do the most good. Yet Democratic leaders in Congress and the Obama administration appear ready to scale back one of the most successful and cost-effective immigration law enforcement programs ever launched.

al Enforcement Gets the Job Done

his program, known as 287(g), allows police, sheriffs, and other local law enforcement agencies to provide direct assistance to federal agents in identifying illegal alien criminals and putting them on the path to removal from the country. By expediting the removal of foreign lawbreakers, 287(g) saves taxpayers money.

Its cost: about $60 million over the last three fiscal years. In contrast, ICE spent more than ten times that annual cost— about $219 million—last year alone to remove 34,000 aliens under the fugitive operations program. There are local benefits, too; the Arizona Department of Public Safety saved nearly $3 million in incarceration costs in just the first year.

Currently, illegal aliens who make it past border patrol agents, consular officers and port of entry inspectors are largely home free. ICE has just a few thousand agents, concentrated in cities, to deal with a widely scattered illegal population that recently reached 12 million, including nearly seven million in the work force and as many as 400,000 in jails and prisons. This mismatch works well for illegal aliens, especially the criminals.

For a long time, local communities have been stuck with the economic and social consequences. But in 1996, Congress heeded their pleas and gave them this tool to address public safety problems associated with illegal immigration and help out the feds at the same time. State and local law agencies who sign up get advanced training for selected officers, access to immigration databases, and authority to seek removal for criminal aliens.

Interest soared after 9/11, and, since 2006, officers in the program have identified about 90,000 criminal aliens. According to ICE documents we obtained through the Freedom of Information Act for a forthcoming report, 287(g) arrests represented about one-fifth of all ICE criminal alien arrests in 2008. All of the removable aliens were identified by trained officers in the regular course of their duties in corrections, highway patrol, or criminal investigations. They include murderers, rapists, gangsters, drunk drivers, and even a few suspected terrorists.

The demand for the program is the best testament to its popularity. Sixty-seven jurisdictions are now taking part, and another 42 are on the waiting list.

Opponents of Enforcement

The program's success has made it a prime target of anti-immigration enforcement advocacy groups. The ACLU, Appleseed Network, and allies for years have denounced the program, published breathless reports, and launched campaigns to help local activists thwart its adoption in their communities. Opponents in Congress recently commissioned a GAO report, and on March 4, House Homeland Security Committee Chair Bennie Thompson convened a three-hour hearing to investigate alleged ICE mismanagement of the program.

Congressional leaders need to resist any moves to stifle local involvement in immigration law enforcement.

Detractors complain that 287(g) officers identify mainly "minor" criminals and that they often are abusing their authority. At the hearing, Muzaffar Chishti, of the Migration Policy Institute, noted with alarm that many of the 287(g) jurisdictions were in the Southeast, and sought to link these communities' concern about illegal alien crime to what he called their "troubled legacy of civil rights violations and racial profiling," wink, wink. Critics demand that ICE rein in the locals by establishing tighter guidelines, including a requirement that only "serious" criminals be charged with immigration violations, and that only correctional institutions be allowed to participate.

Such hysterics are to be expected from the usual suspects, but are a little unusual from the GAO. Their report dinged ICE for an apparent lack of "documented program objectives" that would provide a true measure of success. What the GAO inexplicably missed is that Congress created this program to serve primarily local objectives, not ICE objectives. California sheriffs use the program to have illegal alien felons and gangsters removed. In Florida, they target suspects in homeland security investigations. In Alabama, one focus is on preventing driver's license fraud. The Colorado state patrol uses the program to combat human smuggling on the highways. In South Carolina, the problem is bogus documents in the work place. In Massachusetts, it's drug dealing and gangs. ICE should not have to force local agencies, who are the best judge of what local problems are, into a one-size-fits-all program. And, since not all criminal aliens are in jails, the task force, investigative and highway patrol options must be preserved.

As for racial profiling and abuse of authority, even the GAO could not turn up even a single instance.

The move to narrow the scope of the 287(g) program is wrapped up in concerns about program management but really boils down to a control issue. Key Democratic lawmakers and the Obama administration have signaled that they intend to minimize immigration law enforcement, thus preserving the status quo of a de facto amnesty for those who breach the borders. Congressional leaders need to resist any moves to stifle local involvement in immigration law enforcement and preserve local agencies' ability to address immigration-related public safety problems in their community.

11

Illegal Immigrants Should Not Be Able to Get Driver's Licenses

Numbers USA

Numbers USA is an organization that works to promote lower immigration levels to the United States.

Driver's licenses and identification cards are used to establish legitimacy and open up doors of opportunity for those who have them. Issuing these forms of identification to illegal immigrants allows them to gain access to services and gives their presence legitimacy. Many states currently allow people to get driver's licenses and identification cards without adequate proof of legal residence. Despite the claims to the contrary, granting driver's licenses to illegal aliens will not improve the safety of the roads, as they will still be unlikely to buy insurance or interact with law enforcement. Because there are many reasons for illegal immigrants to give false information to obtain driver's licenses, granting them would threaten national security.

State-issued driver's licenses and identification cards open doors of opportunity in the United States. Not only does the driver's license grant Americans the privilege to operate a vehicle, it also is widely accepted as an identification card that enables the bearer to access a plethora of services and benefits. Driver's licenses and ID cards are used to rent apartments and cars, open bank accounts, cash checks, enter secure buildings, buy guns, and board commercial aircraft, among other things.

"Rewards for Illegal Aliens—Driver's Licenses," *Numbers USA*, December 4, 2007. Reproduced by permission.

Acceptance of these documents as proof of identity has become so commonplace in America that presenting a different document, like a passport, may attract attention and lead to increased scrutiny, even if the alternative document is actually more secure. This is why driver's licenses and ID cards are so valuable to terrorists and illegal aliens, who use them to hide in plain sight without attracting unwanted attention. As the 9/11 Commission noted in its final report, reliable identification is vital for security reasons. Fraudulent licenses and IDs "complicated the government's ability to adequately ensure public safety at vulnerable facilities including airport terminals, train stations, bus stations, and other entry points."

Driver's licenses and ID cards are particularly valuable to illegal aliens since they are accepted as proof of identity on the I-9 form employers are required to complete to establish that new employees are legally eligible to work in the United States. With a driver's license and a stolen or counterfeit social security card, an illegal alien has everything he needs to secure a job and all the other necessities of life in America.

Despite the fact that licenses and ID cards are the identity documents of choice in America, some states are disturbingly careless about to whom they are issued and for how long they remain valid. These two issues—eligibility and duration of validity—largely determine whether illegal aliens are able to obtain licenses and ID cards.

One-third of the estimated 10 million illegal aliens currently residing in the United States are thought to have entered legally and then overstayed their visas, according to DHS [Department of Homeland Security]. Even in states that require proof of lawful presence from applicants, these aliens often are able to obtain licenses and ID cards that expire long after the alien's visa expires. Mohammed Atta, for example, entered the United States on a six-month tourist visa but was issued a Florida driver's license with an expiration date of 09/

01/07—six years after he flew an airplane into the North Tower of the World Trade Center.

Illegal-alien advocacy groups rely on the assertions below to justify the issuance of driver's licenses to illegal aliens. Each appears reasonable on its face, but none holds up under scrutiny.

> Myth 1: Illegal aliens are going to drive no matter what, so issuing them licenses will improve the safety of our roads by ensuring that they have passed a driving test and purchased automobile insurance.

In 2004, automobile accidents resulted in about 42,000 deaths and more than 100,000 injuries in the United States. The vast majority of the people involved in these accidents were licensed, insured drivers, so the correlation asserted by the advocates is tenuous at best. Moreover, most illegal aliens are low-wage workers who send a significant portion of their earnings to their home countries in the form of remittances. They have little incentive to spend their wages on car insurance, and even less incentive to wait for the police to arrive after an accident, since contact with law enforcement authorities could result in deportation. Finally, this suggestion that we just accept the inevitability of illegal aliens' presence in the United States and treat them as lawful residents undermines our belief in law and fairness. No one would suggest that we not lock our doors because burglars are going to break in anyway.

> Myth 2: Law enforcement officials will be better able to track illegal aliens if they are licensed, since their personal data will be entered into driver's license databases.

This claim holds out the promise that law enforcement officials would actually use DMV data to locate and remove illegal aliens. Of course, the very same advocacy groups that use this argument would protest endlessly if such enforcement were proposed. More importantly, though, illegal aliens would not apply for licenses—and certainly would not provide their real names or addresses—if they knew the data would be used to track them. Many already use false names and/or addresses to obtain licenses, just as the 9/11 terrorists who obtained licenses in Virginia did.

> *Myth 3: DMV employees would have to become immigration experts in order to know which documents they can accept as proof of lawful presence.*

It would, in fact, be burdensome if DMV employees had to know which immigration documents are legitimate and which are not. That is precisely why the federal government created the Systematic Alien Verification for Entitlements (SAVE) system. SAVE is an automated system that allows state and local government officials to verify immigration documents. DMV employees would simply have to enter the document number and the name of the bearer into the computer and wait for an answer. Welfare agencies and certain employers have been using the SAVE system for years to verify immigration documents, so there is no reason DMV employees could not use it as well.

In response to the 9/11 attacks, the American Association of Motor Vehicle Administrators (AAMVA) acknowledged the importance of ensuring that state-issued driver's licenses and ID cards are accurate and can be relied upon as proof of the bearer's identity. Betty Serian, Chairwoman of AAMVA's Special Task Force on Identification Security, acknowledged that driver's licenses are much more than just a license to drive. As the most widely accepted identity document, their reliability has a direct affect on homeland security: "When you can verify an individual's identity you are one step closer to preventing fraud, protecting privacy and saving lives."

In post-9/11 America, security is of the utmost importance. There is now a greater need for reliable identification to ensure that our planes, trains, buildings and communities are protected against terrorist threats. The issuance of state ID cards and driver's licenses to illegal aliens undermines our safety. The 9/11 Commission addressed this issue squarely:

> *Secure identification should begin in the United States. The federal government should set standards for the issuance of birth certificates and sources of identification, such as drivers licenses. Fraud in identification documents is no longer just a problem of theft. At many entry points to vulnerable facilities, including gates for boarding aircraft, sources of identification are the last opportunity to ensure that people are who they say they are and to check whether they are terrorists.*

12

Children of Illegal Aliens Should Go to College and Gain Legal Status

David Bennion

David Bennion is an immigration attorney at Nationalities Service Center in Philadelphia, Pennsylvania.

Many students graduate from U.S. high schools with undocumented status—that is, they are not legally permitted to reside in the United States. Many of them were brought to the United States as young children and have lived in America for most of their lives. Once they graduate from high school, there are few opportunities for them as they lack access to in-state college tuition or the legal ability to work. The Development, Relief, and Education for Alien Minors Act, or DREAM Act, would change this, offering undocumented youth the chance at legal resident status. These youths, or Dreamers, should be allowed to have the chance to stay in the country they call home.

Periodically, a young person walks into my office for an initial immigration legal consultation, sometimes accompanied by a parent or other family member, sometimes alone. She speaks with an American accent and tells me how she attended local elementary, junior high and high schools. Perhaps she studied a year or two in college before dropping out for financial reasons or perhaps has only just graduated from high school. To all outward appearances, she is a typical American kid.

David Bennion, "Undocumented Youths Organize to Pass DREAM Act," *Legal Intelligencer*, August 31, 2009, Reproduced by permission.

So why would this young person be sitting in the office of a nonprofit immigration legal services agency like Nationalities Service Center? Because she is undocumented and has no existing remedy for obtaining legal status in the United States. She may even already be in removal (commonly known as deportation) proceedings. She may already have a final order of removal and a "bag and baggage" letter ordering her to present herself to immigration authorities on a date certain to be flown back to her country of birth. She may then be forced to leave behind U.S. citizen parents, siblings or a significant other. She may be exiled from the only country she has ever really known.

Each year, about 65,000 undocumented students graduate from high school in the United States. They then face often insurmountable barriers to pursuing further education or employment opportunities. Many colleges and universities will not permit them to enroll. Even if they are admitted, most financial aid is not available to them. In most states, they will pay prohibitively expensive out-of-state tuition rates, regardless of how long they have lived in the state.

The Development, Relief, and Education for Alien Minors Act, or DREAM Act, is a bill pending in Congress that would provide [to undocumented youths who were brought as children] to the United States ... conditional legal immigration status, [if] they meet certain conditions.

The DREAM Act

To qualify for DREAM Act benefits, an applicant must:

- Have been brought to the United States before age 16.

- Have lived in the United States for at least five years.

- Be a person of good moral character (having not committed any serious crimes).

- Have been admitted to college or earned a high school diploma or GED [general education development degree].

- Serve two years in the military or complete two years of college.

The DREAM Act was first introduced in 2001 but has not yet been passed into law. After the historic immigration marches in 2006 and the subsequent failure of Congress to pass comprehensive immigration reform, Dream Act-eligible students, or Dreamers, mobilized as never before. They are not sitting idly by, waiting for someone to pull them out of their nightmarish situation, as daily immigration home raids and record levels of immigration detention and deportation have continued well into 2009. They connected in new online forums like the Dream Act Portal and *Dreamactivist.org*.

On the Internet, Dreamers found that they were not alone, as many had believed. Online interactions could be anonymous and offered a safe place to talk and organize without fear. Online mobilization translated into offline organizing, and DREAM Act student groups have formed in California, Texas, Florida and New York, among other states.

These students have waited long enough to achieve their own American Dream.

The efforts of the grassroots DREAM Act movement are starting to have a visible effect. The DREAM Act was reintroduced in early 2009 in the House (H.R. 1751) by Representative Howard Berman, D-Calif., and in the Senate (S.729) by Senator Richard Durbin, D-Ill. The act enjoys growing bipartisan support but has become entangled in the broader immigration reform debate. While supporters believe the DREAM Act could pass if a vote were called now [August 2009], the bill is being packaged as a component of forthcoming comprehensive reform legislation.

The Dreamers

In July, for the first time that I am aware, Dreamers mobilized their network to engage Sens. Robert Menendez, D-N.J., and Bill Nelson, D-Fla., to successfully persuade the Department of Homeland Security [DHS] to defer the imminent deportations of two Dreamers. But thousands of Dreamers are deported every year. Ad hoc efforts to stop individual deportations are difficult and do not address the underlying problem that the DHS has so far refused to provide a systemic temporary remedy while the DREAM Act is pending in Congress.

Dreamers are honor students and athletes. They are aspiring schoolteachers, scientists, scholars, lawyers, doctors and social workers. Some want to serve their country abroad. In my experience, they are talented, incredibly engaged and deeply committed to the American nation and their local communities. Many do not speak the language of their home countries. They cannot imagine leaving the country they grew up in, their high school friends, their teachers, coaches and ministers. Some of them were brought as infants or toddlers and cannot remember living anywhere else. Dreamers often cannot find employment because of their unauthorized status. Contrary to conventional wisdom, they cannot obtain legal status by joining the military. In fact, one Dreamer in Missouri was arrested and placed in removal proceedings after attempting to enlist in the armed forces, unaware of his undocumented status. . . .

These students have waited long enough to achieve their own American Dream. Help them make their dreams a reality. Help pass the DREAM Act.

13

Children of Illegal Aliens Should Not Go to College and Gain Legal Status

Yeh Ling-Ling

Yeh Ling-Ling is executive director of the Diversity Alliance for a Sustainable America and herself an immigrant.

Passing the Development, Relief, and Education for Alien Minors Act, or DREAM Act, is a bad idea. Allowing illegal immigrant students to pay in-state college tuition and gain residency would only encourage more illegal immigrants in the United States. The act would have a negative economic impact and hurt American citizens. In addition, this act would lead to serious political impact as immigrants in future years would constitute a sizable population, able to sway elections. America's future prosperity depends upon limiting immigration, and the DREAM Act is in conflict with this goal.

Many leaders of both parties in Congress are pushing for the DREAM Act, which would grant reduced tuition and legal permanent residency to possibly millions of students who have been in the United States illegally. Why is the DREAM Act unfair, irresponsible and disastrous if it is adopted?

The Economic Impact

College tuition has skyrocketed in recent years. Many Americans cannot afford college or have taken out student loans.

Should the United States neglect its own citizens and subsidize the education of students who are here illegally? Proponents of the DREAM Act argue that parents of illegal students have paid taxes and that the United States should invest in them. The hard truth is that most illegal workers, due to their low-incomes, do not pay enough taxes to offset the cost of educating their children in American public grade schools. This cost can exceed $9,500 per child per year if the student receives the so-called bilingual education, not to mention the costs of other social services.

Furthermore, rewarding illegal foreign nationals can only lead to higher illegal immigration. The misnamed "Immigration Reform and Control Act" of 1986 granted amnesty to 3 million illegal migrants. Presently, we have an estimated 12 to 20 million illegal migrants in the United States, without counting their children born here who are U.S. citizens. There were "1.8 million undocumented children in local school districts" across the United States, according to a report published by *Business Week Online*. Billions of bonds in recent years have been passed to fund our schools. Is borrowing into the future a responsible solution?

Open border advocates claim that money spent on the Iraq war and taxing wealthy individuals in the United States could generate plenty of resources to pay for costly services provided to foreign-born newcomers and their U.S.-born children. But the impact of exploding immigration-driven population growth is more than fiscal. If we grant amnesty to millions of illegal students, once naturalized, they could petition for their parents and siblings to immigrate to the United States. In addition, they will have children born here. Those newcomers will consume energy and water, like all other residents, thus exacerbating our energy and water shortages.

The Political Impact

We cannot ignore the political impact of the DREAM Act. Many Hispanic activists pushing for amnesty have publicly stated: "Today, we march. Tomorrow, we vote." During last year's massive demonstrations across the United States, many protestors were waving Mexican flags and pressuring the United States with demands identical to Mexico's. Considering that in recent years, our national elections were very close, it is unlikely that our immigration laws will be seriously enforced in the future if millions of newly naturalized citizens promoting open borders are able to vote in our future elections. Should we allow migration to strongly influence our elections and policies?

American students fall behind their counterparts in many countries in Asia due in part to an explosion of immigration-related enrollments.

The U.S. population has quadrupled since 1900, from 76 million to 303 million. In the last 15 years alone, over 50 million people have been added to the United States mostly due to immigration-derived growth! If our population continues to grow at the rate of last decade, by 2100—within the lifetimes of today's children's children—the United States will have India's current population. Do Asian and Hispanic legal residents really want the United States to become another Latin America, India or Philippines, the corrupt, overpopulated and impoverished nations that they or their ancestors left? Latin America has 37 billionaires. Why shouldn't they and other countries work to improve life for their own citizens?

Congress must realize that the United States is now the greatest debtor nation in human history, while China holds the world's largest foreign currency reserves. We owe China $450 billion in federal debt. We also have the highest budget and trade deficits in the world. The Euro, weaker than the dollar 10 years ago, is now worth over $1.40. American students fall behind their counterparts in many countries in Asia due in part to an explosion of immigration-related enrollments: Many grade schools are overwhelmed with children speaking little to no English. Can this country remain prosperous if we have a growing semi-literate student population?

Nationwide, over 75 percent of our adult cash welfare recipients are 20 to 39 years old. Some growers in Idaho and Colorado are using non-violent prisoners to replace illegal migrants. Isn't it in the interests of Hispanic and other Americans to oppose the DREAM Act and other amnesty proposals, and to demand that our immigration laws be enforced as strictly as Mexico so that we can put all adult able-bodied welfare recipients and non-violent prison inmates to fill positions currently held by illegal migrants?

Organizations to Contact

The editors have compiled the following list of organizations concerned with the issues debated in this book. The descriptions are derived from materials provided by the organizations. All have publications or information available for interested readers. The list was compiled on the date of publication of the present volume; the information provided here may change. Readers need to remember that many organizations take several weeks or longer to respond to inquiries.

American Civil Liberties Union (ACLU)
125 Broad Street, 18th Floor, New York, NY 10004
(212) 549-2500
e-mail: infoaclu@aclu.org
Web site: www.aclu.org

The ACLU is a national organization that works to defend Americans' civil rights as guaranteed in the U.S. Constitution. The ACLU Immigrants' Rights Project is dedicated to expanding and enforcing the civil liberties and civil rights of noncitizens, and to combating public and private discrimination against immigrants. The ACLU publishes the semiannual newsletter *Civil Liberties Alert*, as well as briefing papers including the publication "Immigration Myths and Facts."

American Immigration Council
1331 G Street NW, Suite 200, Washington, DC 20005-3141
(202) 507-7500 • fax (202) 742-5619
Web site: www.americanimmigrationcouncil.org

The American Immigration Council (formerly the American Immigration Law Foundation) is an educational organization that works to strengthen America by honoring its immigrant history. The American Immigration Council promotes humane immigration policies that honor human rights, and it works to achieve fairness for immigrants under the law. It publishes numerous fact sheets and reports through its Immigration Policy Center, including "The Economic Blame Game: U.S. Unemployment Is Not Caused by Immigration."

Americans for Immigration Control (AIC)

PO Box 738, Monterey, VA   24465
(540) 468-2023 • fax (540) 468-2026
e-mail: aic@immigrationcontrol.com
Web site: www.immigrationcontrol.com

AIC is a nonpartisan organization that favors deportation of illegal immigrants and opposes amnesty and guest worker legislation. AIC works to educate and motivate citizens to join efforts to secure America's borders. AIC publishes several books and videos on the topic of immigration, including the 2007 title by AIC spokesman Phil Kent, *What's Yours Is Mine*.

Cato Institute

1000 Massachusetts Ave. NW, Washington, DC   20001-5403
(202) 842-0200 • fax (202) 842-3490
Web site: www.cato.org

The Cato Institute is a public policy research foundation dedicated to limiting the role of government, protecting individual liberties, and promoting free markets. The institute commissions a variety of publications, including books, monographs, briefing papers, and other studies. Among its publications are the quarterly magazine *Regulation*, the bimonthly *Cato Policy Report*, and articles such as "Keeping Racism Alive."

Center for Immigration Studies

1522 K Street NW, Suite 820, Washington, DC   20005-1202
(202) 466-8185 • fax (202) 466-8076
e-mail: center@cis.org
Web site: www.cis.org

The Center for Immigration Studies is an independent research organization devoted exclusively to research and policy analysis of the economic, social, demographic, fiscal, and other impacts of immigration on the United States. The Center for Immigration Studies is animated by a unique pro-immigrant, low-immigration vision that seeks fewer immigrants but a warmer welcome for those admitted. The Center for Immigration Studies publishes reports, memos, and opinion pieces available at its Web site, including "Immigration and Crime: Assessing a Conflicted Issue."

Federation for American Immigration Reform (FAIR)

25 Massachusetts Ave. NW, Suite 330, Washington, DC   20001
(877) 627-3247
e-mail: comments@fairus.org
Web site: www.fairus.org

FAIR is a nonprofit organization of concerned citizens who share a common belief that the nation's immigration policies must be reformed to serve the national interest. FAIR seeks to improve border security, to stop illegal immigration, and to promote immigration levels at rates around 300,000 a year. FAIR publishes briefs and reports on immigration issues, including the report, "Amnesty and Joblessness: Unemployed Americans Shouldn't Have to Compete for Jobs with Illegal Aliens."

Migration Policy Institute (MPI)

1400 16th Street NW, Suite 300, Washington, DC   20036
(202) 266-1940 • fax (202) 266-1900
e-mail: info@migrationpolicy.org
Web site: www.migrationpolicy.org

MPI is an independent, nonpartisan think tank dedicated to the study of the movement of people worldwide. MPI provides analysis, development, and evaluation of migration and refugee policies at the local, national, and international levels. MPI publishes books, reports, and fact sheets, including the policy brief "Immigration Enforcement: Beyond the Border and the Workplace."

National Immigration Forum

50 F Street NW, Suite 300, Washington, DC   20001
(202) 347-0040 • fax (202) 347-0058
Web site: www.immigrationforum.org

The National Immigration Forum is an organization that advocates for the value of immigrants and immigration to the nation. The National Immigration Forum works to foster immigration policy that honors American ideals, protects human dignity, reflects the economic demands of the United States, celebrates family unity, and provides opportunities for progress. The Forum publishes numerous backgrounders, fact sheets, and issue papers, including "Assets or Enemies: Securing our Nation by Enforcing Immigration Laws."

National Immigration Law Center (NILC)

3435 Wilshire Blvd., Suite 2850, Los Angeles, CA   90010
(213) 639-3900 • fax (213) 639-3911
e-mail: irwin@nilc.org
Web site: www.nilc.org

NILC is dedicated to protecting and promoting the rights of low-income immigrants and their family members. NILC engages in policy advocacy, impact litigation, and education to secure fair treatment in the courts for immigrants, preserve a safety net for immigrants, and open opportunities for immigrants. NILC publishes manuals and analyses for nonprofit agencies working on immigration issues, including *Immigrants' Rights Update*, a newsletter focused on changes in policy, legislation, and case law affecting low-income immigrants.

National Network for Immigrant and Refugee Rights (NNIRR)

310 8th Street, Suite 303, Oakland, CA   94607
(510) 465-1984 • fax (510) 465-1885
e-mail: nnirr@nnirr.org
Web site: www.nnirr.org

NNIRR is a national organization that serves as a forum to share information and analysis, to educate communities and the general public, and to develop and coordinate plans of action on important immigrant and refugee issues. NNIRR works to promote a just immigration and refugee policy in the United States, and to defend and expand the rights of all immigrants and refugees, regardless of immigration status. NNIRR publishes fact sheets and reports, including the report "Guilty by Immigration Status."

NumbersUSA Action
1601 N Kent Street, Suite 1100, Arlington, VA 22209
(703) 816-8820
Web site: www.numbersusa.com

NumbersUSA is a nonprofit, nonpartisan, public policy organization that favors an environmentally sustainable and economically just America. NumbersUSA opposes efforts to use federal immigration policies to force mass U.S. population growth and to depress wages of vulnerable workers. NumbersUSA publishes fact sheets, including "Putting Americans Back to Work?"

U.S. Citizenship and Immigration Service (USCIS)
425 I Street NW, Washington, DC 20536
(800) 375-5283
Web site: www.uscis.gov

USCIS is the government agency that oversees lawful immigration to the United States. USCIS provides immigration information, grants immigration and citizenship benefits, promotes an awareness and understanding of citizenship, and ensures the integrity of the U.S. immigration system. USCIS provides numerous reports, informational resources, and immigration forms, including "Mandatory Verification in the States: A Policy Research Agenda."

U.S. Immigration and Customs Enforcement (ICE)
500 12th Street SW, Washington, DC 20536
Web site: www.ice.gov

ICE is the largest investigative agency in the U.S. Department of Homeland Security (DHS). ICE's mission is to protect the security of the American people and homeland by vigilantly enforcing the nation's immigration and customs laws. ICE publishes the quarterly *Cornerstone Report*, fact sheets, and reports.

Bibliography

Books

David Bacon	*Illegal People: How Globalization Creates Migration and Criminalizes Immigrants*. Boston, MA: Beacon Press, 2008.
Justin Akers Chacon and Mike Davis	*No One Is Illegal: Fighting Violence and State Repression on the U.S.-Mexico Border*. Chicago: Haymarket Books, 2006.
Aviva Chomsky	*"They Take Our Jobs!": And 20 Other Myths About Immigration*. Boston, MA: Beacon Press, 2007.
Jane Guskin and David L. Wilson	*The Politics of Immigration: Questions and Answers*. New York: Monthly Review Press, 2007.
J.D. Hayworth	*Whatever It Takes: Illegal Immigration, Border Security, and the War on Terror*. Washington, DC: Regnery, 2006.
Bill Ong Hing	*Deporting Our Souls: Values, Morality, and Immigration Policy*. New York: Cambridge University Press, 2006.
James K. Hoffmeier	*The Immigration Crisis: Immigrants, Aliens, and the Bible*. Wheaton, IL: Crossway Books, 2009.

Kevin R. Johnson   *Opening the Floodgates: Why America Needs to Rethink Its Borders and Immigration Laws.* New York: New York University Press, 2007.

Mark Krikorian   *The New Case Against Immigration: Both Legal and Illegal.* New York: Sentinel, 2008.

Heather Mac Donald, Victor Davis Hanson, and Steven Malanga   *The Immigration Solution: A Better Plan than Today's.* Chicago: Ivan R. Dee, 2007.

Nicolaus Mills   *Arguing Immigration: The Debate over the Changing Face of America.* New York: Simon & Schuster, 2007.

Lina Newton   *Illegal, Alien, or Immigrant: The Politics of Immigration Reform.* New York: New York University Press, 2008.

Carol M. Swain, ed.   *Debating Immigration.* New York: Cambridge University Press, 2007.

Tom Tancredo   *In Mortal Danger: The Battle for America's Border and Security.* Nashville, TN: WND Books, 2006.

Helen Thorpe   *Just Like Us: The True Story of Four Mexican Girls Coming of Age in America.* New York: Scribner, 2009.

Periodicals

Sasha Abramsky   "Gimme Shelter," *Nation*, February 25, 2008.

America   "Migration, the Larger Picture," January 7, 2008.

David Bacon   "Railroading Immigrants," *Nation*, October 6, 2008.

Michael Barone   "Why Enforcement Matters," *U.S. News & World Report*, June 4, 2007.

George R. Boggs   "Why Congress Should Revive the Dream Act," *Chronicle of Higher Education*, March 28, 2008.

William F. Buckley, Jr.   "Illegalizing Illegals," *National Review*, November 3, 2007.

Megan Eckstein   "In-State Tuition for Undocumented Students: Not Quite Yet," *Chronicle of Higher Education*, May 8, 2009.

Economist   "Not Very NICE," April 26, 2008.

Alan Greenblatt   "Immigration Debate," *CQ Researcher*, February 1, 2008.

Larry Greenley   "How to Fix Illegal Immigration," *New American*, March 3, 2008.

Daniel Griswold   "Immigration Law Should Reflect Our Dynamic Labor Market," *Dallas Morning News*, April 27, 2008.

Jim Harper — "Electronic Employment Eligibility Verification: Franz Kafka's Solution to Illegal Immigration," *Policy Analysis*, March 6, 2008.

John B. Judis — "Phantom Menace: The Psychology Behind America's Immigration Hysteria," *New Republic*, February 13, 2008.

John F. Kavanaugh — "Amnesty? Let Us Be Vigilant and Charitable," *America*, March 10, 2008.

Tom Knott — "Dream Act Begins an American Nightmare," *Washington Times*, October 11, 2007.

Kris W. Kobach — "A Sleeper Amnesty: Time to Wake Up from the DREAM Act," *Backgrounder #2069*, September 13, 2007. www.heritage.org.

Mark Krikorian — "No Amnesty—Now or in Two Years," *National Review Online*, October 31, 2008. www.nationalreview.com.

William McKenzie — "Why Dream Act Makes Sense for Illegal Immigrants—and Our Country," *Dallas Morning News*, September 29, 2009.

John F. McManus — "The Battle Against Illegal Immigration," *New American*, March 3, 2008.

Stephanie Mencimer — "Texas Hold 'em: The Lucrative Business of Locking Up Immigrants," *Mother Jones*, July-August 2008.

What Rights Should Illegal Immigrants Have?

Ruben Navarrette, Jr.	"Laws and Borders," *Hispanic*, February-March 2009.

Charles Scaliger	"Avoiding Extreme Solutions," *New American*, March 3, 2008.

Peter Schrag	"Divided States," *Nation*, January 7, 2008.

Emma Schwartz	"A Bust, and a Blow to a Business," *U.S. News & World Report*, October 1, 2007.

Beth Schwartzapfel	"Held in Purgatory," *Ms.*, Summer 2009.

Geri Smith and Keith Epstein	"On the Border: The 'Virtual Fence' Isn't Working," *BusinessWeek*, February 18, 2008.

Nathan Thornburgh	"Undocumented and Undeterred," *Time*, April 20, 2009.

Washington Times	"End the Dream," October 24, 2007.

Index

A

Adult illiteracy, 24, 25
AFL-CIO (American Federation of Labor and Congress of Industrial Organizations), 30, 31
African Americans, 50
Agricultural workers, 63
AgriProcessors plant raid, 45–50
Alabama, 74
Alexiev, Alex, 23–28
American Association of Motor Vehicle Administrators (AAMVA), 78
American Civil Liberties Union (ACLU), 43, 73, 88
Americans for Tax Reform, 47
Amnesty
    Bush administration and, 37
    de facto amnesty, 62
    meaning, 60
    Obama and, 27
    open borders and, 45, 47
    opposition, 9, 51–58, 64
    political disagreement, 9, 48, 49, 60
    public opinion polls and, 49
    S1639 (Bush-Kennedy Amnesty Bill), 48, 49
Appleseed Networks, 73
Arizona, 18–20, 72
Army Corps of Engineers, 17
Arrests, 40, 41
Asian immigrants, 24
Associated Press (AP), 34
Atta, Mohammed, 76
Auto insurance, 77

B

Background checks, 69
Bacon, David, 29–33, 41, 43
Baksh, Stokely, 42
Bennion, David, 80–83
Berman, Howard, 82
Birth certificates, 79
Border (U.S./Mexico)
    Department of Homeland Security and, 18–19
    fencing, 19
    Mexican drug cartels and, 71
    Operation Blockade, 19–21
    Operation Gatekeeper, 20
    Operation Streamline, 18, 20
    securitization, 11, 12, 13, 17–19, 22
    surveillance, 19
    U.S. Border Patrol agents, 19
Borjas, George J., 27
Brazil, 36
Bureau of Labor Statistics (BLS), 52, 55, 56, 66
Bush, George W., 18–19, 30, 36, 37, 48, 55
Bush-Kennedy Amnesty Bill (S1639), 48, 49
The Business of Detention (Feltz and Baksh), 42
BusinessWeek Online, 85

C

California
    DREAM Act and, 82
    Operation Gatekeeper and, 20

problems caused by illegal
immigration, 23–28
raids, 14
student population, 24
287(g) program and, 74
underground economy, 25
California Dropout Research
Project, 24
Camp, Jim, 39
Canadian Labour Congress, 31
CBP (U.S. Customs and Border
Protection), 12
Center for Immigration Studies,
38, 48
Change to Win unions, 30, 32
Chertoff, Michael, 18
Child labor, 46
Children of illegal immigrants
college education and, 80–87
costs of public education, 27,
85
deportation of parents and, 68
raids and, 15
right to education, 8
China, 86
Chishti, Muzaffar, 73
Clinton, Bill, 19
Coalicion de Derechos Humanos,
19
Colleges and universities
attendance rates, 25–26
DREAM Act, 9, 80–87
emigration from California
and, 25–26
illegal aliens and, 80–87
Latinos and, 24
shortage of graduates, 25
student loans, 9, 81, 84–85
tuition rates, 9

unemployment rates and,
56–57
See also Education
Colorado, 74, 87
Connecticut, 14
Construction industry, 48
Corrections Corporation of
America (CCA), 16, 42
Cuba, 68

D

DeCosse, David, 59–64
Del Bosque, Melissa, 43
Deportation
automobile accidents and, 77
"bag and baggage" letter, 81
controversy, 9
deportations in 2006, 13
earned legalization and, 65–70
illegal aliens as criminals,
71–74
self-deportation, 48
DeStefano, John Jr., 15
Detention
facilities, 17
health care and, 42–43
mandatory detention, 16
private prison firms and, 12,
16, 42
statistics 1994 and 2006, 16
Development, Relief, and Education for Alien Minors Act
(DREAM Act), 9, 80–87
DHS. *See* U.S. Department of
Homeland Security
Dobbs, Lou, 43
Doe, Plyler v., 8–9
DREAM Act, 9, 80–87
Dreamactivist.org, 82
Driver's licenses, 9, 74–79

Dropouts, 24, 57
Drug trafficking, 39, 71, 74
Durbin, Richard, 82

E

E-Verify, 30, 37
Earned legalization, 65–70
Economic downturn, 48
Education
    children of illegal immigrants,
        9, 80–87
    costs of education, 27, 85
    dropouts, 24
    exploitation of workers and,
        46
    illegal immigrant adults, 24,
        27, 47, 57
    in-state tuition rates, 9
    litigation, 8–9
    non-English speaking stu-
        dents, 87
    school lunch programs, 39
    student loans, 9, 81, 84–85
    unemployment and, 56–57
    work-study programs, 9
    See also Colleges and univer-
        sities
Edwards, James, 71–74
El Salvador, 14, 36
Ellis Island, 61
Employee Free Choice Act, 33
Employer sanctions for hiring ille-
    gal immigrants
    opposition, 29–33
    Sensenbrenner bill and, 12–13
    support for, 27
Energy shortages, 85
Equal Protection Clause of Four-
    teenth Amendment, 9

F

Family Security Matters, 39
Federal debt, 86
Federation for American Immigra-
    tion Reform (FAIR), 7
Feltz, Renee, 42
Fennelly, Katherine, 65–70
Fencing U.S./Mexico border, 19
Florida, 74, 76–77, 82, 83
Food Stamps, 39
Food transport, 13
Fourteenth Amendment, 9
Fourth Amendment, 13
Fox News, 37
Fraud
    driver's licenses, 74, 76, 78
    forged Green Cards, 46
    identity theft, 13, 36
    Social Security numbers, 13,
        36
Freedom of Information Act, 72
Friedman, Milton, 28
FrontPage Magazine, 45–46

G

Gangs, 73, 74
Geo Group, 16
Georgetti, Ken, 31
Germany, 36
Glazov, Jamie, 45–50
Globalization, 31
Goldstein, Amy, 42–43
Gonzalez, Elian, 68
Green cards, 46
Guatemala, 14, 36
Guest workers, 30, 33, 41, 51–52,
    55–57, 63
Gutierrez, Carlos, 18

H

Halliburton, 17
Harper, Stephen, 31
Harris, Stan, 36
Harvard University, 27
Hatch, Patricia, 65–70
Health care for illegal immigrants, 27, 39, 42–43
Hewlett Foundation, 26
Hoar, William P., 34–39
Homeward Bound: Recent Immigration Enforcement and the Decline in the Illegal Alien Population (Center for Immigration Studies), 48
Honduras, 14, 36
Housing, 50
Howard Industries, 41
Hubbard, Enrique, 38
Human capital, 23
Human Rights Immigrant Community Action Network (HURRICANE), 21

I

I-9 forms, 76
ICE. *See* U.S. Immigration and Customs Enforcement (ICE)
Idaho, 87
Identity theft, 13, 36
IFCO Systems, 13
Illegal immigrants
    amnesty and, 9, 37, 48, 49, 51–58
    children of, 8, 15, 27, 68, 80–87
    criminality, 7, 71–74
    driver's licenses and, 74, 75–79

earned legalization, 65–70
education levels, 27, 46, 47, 57
ethical considerations, 59–64
illiteracy, 24, 25
incarceration, 39, 72
myths, 26–27
population statistics, 76
public assistance programs and, 27
rights, 11–22
taxpayer-funded benefits, 8
terrorism and, 16
unemployment, 27, 38
visa expiration, 7
Illegal Immigration Reform and Immigrant Responsibility Act (IIRIRA), 16
Illiteracy, 24, 25
Immigration, 56
Immigration and African-American Employment (National Bureau of Economic Research), 50
Immigration reform, 9, 37, 48, 49, 51–58, *See also* Deportation; Raids
Immigration Reform and Control Act of 1986, 85
Immigration Study of LWVUS, 66, 68
In These Times, 41
Incarceration, 39, 72
Independent Weekly, 42
India, 86
INS (U.S. Immigration and Naturalization Service), 16
Internet, 82
Iowa, 41, 44, 45–50, 54
Iraq, 17, 85
Ireland, 14

IRS (Internal Revenue Service), 26
IT World, 36

J

Jaarda, Christopher M., 51–58
Jobs, 52
The Jungle (Sinclair), 46

K

Kellogg Brown & Root, 17
Kersh, Rogan, 53–54
King, Steve, 54
Krikorian, Mark, 38

L

Labor Notes, 41
Ling-Ling, Yeh, 84–87
Los Angeles Unified School District (CA), 24
LWVUS (League of Women Voters of the United States), 66

M

Maestretti, Danielle, 40–44
Manhattan Institute, 27
Markkula Center for Applied Ethics at Santa Clara University, 60
Martinez-Mendez, Juan Carlos, 43
Massachusetts, 14, 67, 74
Mayorga, Jessica, 15
McCain, John, 37, 47
McCain-Kennedy immigration reform bill, 68
Meatpacking industry, 13, 31
Medicare, 69
Menendez, Robert, 83

Mexico
drug cartels, 71
illegal immigrants in U.S. and, 14, 36, 61, 86
immigration laws, 87
poverty, 29, 31
welfare programs, 28, 37
See also Border (U.S./Mexico)
Michael Bianco, Inc., 14
Migration Policy Institute, 73
Mississippi, 35, 36, 40, 41
Missouri, 83
Mother Jones, 42
Multi-City Study of Urban Inequality, 50
Myers, Julie, 67

N

NAFTA (North American Free Trade Agreement), 19–20, 22, 31–32
Nation, 41
National Assessment of Education Progress (NAEP), 25
National Bureau of Economic Research, 50
National Center for Higher Education Management Systems, 26
National Immigration Forum, 8
National Immigration Justice Center, 16
National Network for Immigrant and Refugee Rights, 11–22
National Research Council of the American Academy of Sciences, 50
Nationalities Service Center, 81
Nelson, Bill, 83
New America Media, 44

New Americans: Economic, Demographic and Fiscal Effects of Immigrants (National Research Council of the American Academy of Sciences), 50
New Jersey, 83
New York, 53, 82
New York Times, 35, 36
New York University, 53
9/11 terrorist attacks, 16, 64, 72, 76, 77, 78
Norquist, Grover, 47
North American Free Trade Agreement (NAFTA), 19–20, 22, 31–32
North Carolina, 33, 42
Numbers USA, 75–79

O

Obama, Barack
    amnesty program, 27
    correspondence regarding immigration policies, 31–32
    immigration enforcement reduction, 54, 74
    immigration reform and, 30, 37, 43, 51–52, 71
    stimulus package, 52
Obama, Michelle, 34, 35
Oklahoma, 26
Ong Hing, Bill, 29–33
Operation Blockade, 19–21
Operation Endgame, 13
Operation Scheduled Departure, 36–37
Operation Streamline, 18

P

Panama, 36
Peru, 36
Pew Hispanic Center, 7, 27, 57

Pew Research Center, 7
Phoenix New Times, 42
Plyler v. Doe, 8–9
Population growth, 85
Poverty, 29, 31, 45, 47, 63
Priest, Dana, 42–43
Prisons, 27, 39, 42
Public assistance programs, 27, 39

R

Raids
    Bush and, 30, 48
    children of illegal immigrants and, 15
    factory raids, 67
    homes, 12
    IFCO raids, 14
    illegal immigrants as criminals, 40–44
    immigration sweeps, 12
    increase, 11
    justification, 34–39, 45–50
    liberal response, 47–48
    meatpacking plants, 13, 30, 46–47
    negative effect, 11
    positive effect, 45–50
    statistics on arrests, 40–41
    workplace, 13, 15, 30, 67
Raimondi, Marc, 15
Rojas, Ismael, 31
Russia, 14

S

S1639 (Bush-Kennedy Amnesty Bill), 48, 49
San Antonio Current, 43
San Antonio Express-News, 36
Santa Clara University, 60
Schumer, Charles, 52, 53, 54

Seattle Weekly, 43
Self-deportation, 48
Senate Judiciary Committee, 53
Sensenbrenner bill (HR 4437), 12–13
Serian, Betty, 78
Service Processing Centers, 16
Sex crimes, 17, 39
Sinclair, Upton, 46
Smithfield, 33
Social conflict, 50
Social Security numbers
   E-Verify and, 30, 37
   fraud, 13, 36
   immigration status verification, 33
South Carolina, 40, 74
Steinlight, Stephen, 46
Student loans, 9, 81, 84–85
Sweeney, John, 31
"Swift" raids, 13, 31
Systematic Alien Verification for Entitlements (SAVE), 78–79

T

Taxes, 69, 85
Taxpayer-funded benefits, 8
Terrorism, 16, 64, 71, 73, 76
Texas, 8–9, 18, 20–21, 26, 43, 82
Texas Observer, 43
Truthout.org, 43
Tuition rates, 9
287(g) program, 42, 71–74

U

Underclass, 27
Underground economy, 25
Unemployment, 27, 38, 49–50, 51–57

United Food and Commercial Workers Union, 13, 31
United States/Mexico border. *See* Border (U.S./Mexico)
University of California Santa Barbara, 24
Urban Institute, 66–67
U.S. Bureau of Labor Statistics (BLS), 52, 55, 56, 66
U.S. Census Bureau, 38
U.S. Congress, 16
U.S. Constitution, 9, 13
U.S. Customs and Border Protection (CBP), 12
U.S. Department of Homeland Security (DHS)
   budget, 12, 67
   DREAM Act and, 83
   illegal alien population estimate, 76
   Operation Blockade, 19–21
   Operation Endgame, 13
   Operation Scheduled Departure, 36–37
   Operation Streamline, 18, 20
   U.S./Mexico border securitization, 12, 13, 18–19
U.S. Department of Justice, 16, 35, 36
U.S. Government Accountability Office (GAO), 32, 74
U.S. House of Representatives, 12–13
U.S. Immigration and Customs Enforcement (ICE)
   audit of detention centers, 17
   deportations, 67
   IFCO raids, 14
   Operation Scheduled Departure, 37
   287(g) program, 42

vilification of, 47–48
workplace raids, 12, 15, 31, 45–50
U.S. Immigration and Naturalization Service (INS), 16
U.S. Internal Revenue Service (IRS), 26
U.S. Office of the Inspector General, 17
U.S. Senate, 53
U.S. Supreme Court, 8–9

V

Vaughan, Jessica, 71–74
Violent crimes, 39, 71, 73

Virginia, 78
Visa expiration, 7

W

Wackenhut Corrections Corporation, 16
Wages, 37, 50, 77
Washington Post, 17, 42
Water shortages, 85
Weil, Simone, 61
Welfare programs, 27, 39, 78, 87
Work-study programs, 9
Working conditions, 50